Primary Music Box

Traditional songs and activities for younger learners

Sab Will with Susannah Reed

CAMBRIDGE
UNIVERSITY PRESS

CAMBRIDGE UNIVERSITY PRESS
Cambridge, New York, Melbourne, Madrid, Cape Town, Singapore, São Paulo, Delhi, Dubai, Tokyo, Mexico City

Cambridge University Press
The Edinburgh Building, Cambridge CB2 8RU, UK

www.cambridge.org
Information on this title: www.cambridge.org/9780521728560

First published 2010
Reprinted 2010

Printed in the United Kingdom at the University Press, Cambridge

A catalogue record for this publication is available from the British Library

ISBN 978-0-521-72856-0 Paperback

Cambridge University Press has no responsibility for the persistence or accuracy of URLs for external or third-party internet websites referred to in this publication, and does not guarantee that any content on such websites is, or will remain, accurate or appropriate. Information regarding prices, travel timetables and other factual information given in this work is correct at the time of first printing but Cambridge University Press does not guarantee the accuracy of such information thereafter.

Thanks and Acknowledgements

Authors' thanks

The authors would like to thank the editors Liane Grainger and Lynne Rushton for their contribution to this book.

Dedications

Sab Will: For Angelina Misty – my own little song angel
Susannah Reed: Thanks to Ellie and Ben for their inspiration

KOOKABURRA SITS IN THE OLD GUM TREE
Words and Music by Marion Sinclair
© Copyright 1934 and Renewed 1989
Larrikin Music Publishing Pty Ltd. 4/30-32 Carrington St, Sydney NSW 2000 Australia.
All Rights Reserved. International Copyright Secured.
Reprinted by Permission of Campbell Connelly & Co. Limited.

THE HOKEY COKEY
Words and Music by James B Kennedy
© Copyright 1942 Kennedy Music Company Limited.
All rights administered by Campbell Connelly & Co. Limited.
All Rights Reserved. International Copyright Secured.
Reprinted by Permission of Campbell Connelly & Co. Limited.

The authors and publishers would like to thank the following reviewers:

Fiona Dunbar, Bonnie Kennedy, Roz Mays, Pippa Mayfield, Cristina Quincy Avilés, Kate Ruttle, Petra Smythe, Melanie Williams

The authors and publishers are grateful to the following illustrators:

Beccy Blake, Peter Curry, Evelyne Duverne, Clare Elsom, Cathy Hughs, Kamae Design, Bethan Matthews, Stephanie Strickland, Theresa Tibbetts, Matt Ward, Lisa Williams

The publishers are grateful to the following contributors:

Page layout and cover design: Kamae Design
Cover illustration: Graham Ross
Audio production and music arrangements: Tim Woolf

Contents

Level 1	Age	Language covered	Worksheet activities	Follow-up activities
1.1 Ten in the bed	6–7	numbers 1–10, bedroom furniture, personal possessions, prepositions of place *in, on, in front of, between, next to, behind, under*	• Making finger puppets • Putting objects in a bedroom	• Playing Numbers Bingo • Drawing 'My ideal bedroom'
1.2 The wheels on the bus	6–8	transport, sounds on a bus, *Do you go by … ? Yes I do, No I don't*	• Ordering the song and learning actions • Class survey on types of transport used by pupils	• Snap or Pelmanism • Making transport posters
1.3 Hickory dickory dock	6–7	numbers 1–12, o'clock, *What time is it?, It's …, What time do you … ?, I … at … o'clock,* daily routines	• Making a clock and a mouse • Class survey on daily routines	• Making a picture timetable of pupils' daily activities • Time Bingo or Pelmanism
1.4 Dingle dangle scarecrow	6–8	things on a farm, parts of the body	• Using pictures to follow the storyline • Making a scarecrow • Picture dictation	• Singing the song about other parts of the body • Comparing the town and the country
1.5 The music man	6–8	musical instruments, *Can you/he/she … ? I can …*	• 'Join the dots' round musical instruments • Learning about different musical instrument 'families'	• Miming instruments • Adding new instruments to the song
1.6 We wish you a Merry Christmas	6–8	features and customs of a traditional Christmas	• Spot the difference • Making Christmas decorations	• Picture dictation • Drawing food for a special day

Level 1	Age	Language covered	Worksheet activities	Follow-up activities
1.7 Bingo	7–8	the alphabet, spelling	• Spelling Bingo • Spelling games	• Singing the song with new names for the dog • Making a classroom word snake
1.8 Old Macdonald had a farm	7–8	farm animals, animal sounds, animal products	• Matching animals and their sounds • Making a chart showing what animals give us	• Playing 'Guess the animal' • Creating a poster ranking farm animals according to size
1.9 If you're happy and you know it	7–8	parts of the body and actions *If you're ... , + imperative*	• 'Parts of the body' game • Class survey on 'What makes you happy?'	• Labelling body parts • Creating a poster based on a class survey of favourite things
1.10 There was an old lady	7–8	animals and what they eat	• Linking the animals in the old lady's 'meal' • Making the characters in the song • Making 'What do animals eat?' posters	• Picture dictation • Designing a healthy diet
1.11 Here we go round the mulberry bush	7–8	days of the week, daily activities, parts of the body, clothes	• Writing about daily routines • Creating pictures of funnily-dressed people	• Adapting the song • Writing a description of a funnily-dressed person
1.12 There was a princess long ago	7–8	fairy tales	• Ordering the pictures in the song • Making a crown	• Snap • Acting out a fairy tale

Level 2	Age	Language covered	Worksheet activities	Follow-up activities
2.1 The Hokey Cokey	7–10	parts of the body and actions	• Circling pictures in the song chorus and ordering the song • 'Body' crossword puzzle	• Simon Says • Exploring the senses
2.2 Kookaburra	8–10	Australian animals and geographical features, describing animals *It's got …*, *It can …*	• Ordering pictures and completing the song words • Completing animal fact cards	• Playing 'Guess the animal' • Creating animal fact cards
2.3 This old man	8–10	words which rhyme with numbers *1–10*, 'pet' words	• Matching rhyming words and pictures • Rhyming words maze • Doing a 'pets' survey	• Finding rhymes with 'colour' words • Project on pets and looking after them
2.4 We've got the whole world in our hands	8–10	people close to us, nature, towns and cities, rubbish and recycling	• Gap-filling things in the world • Categorising rubbish for recycling	• Project on beautiful places in the world • Keeping a two-day 'recycling' diary
2.5 Do your ears hang low?	8–10	parts of the body, actions, *can* for ability	• Ordering the lines in the song • Survey on funny things you can do	• Creating own survey questions • Class talent show
2.6 I found a peanut	8–10	food and food hygiene, past simple tense and question forms	• Matching questions and answers in the song • Finding food items hidden in a picture	• Making a new version of the song with different answers to the questions • Creating a food safety poster

Level 2	Age	Language covered	Worksheet activities	Follow-up activities
2.7 She'll be coming round the mountain	8–10	*She'll …, She'll be … ing, going to* future, question words *How, What, Where, Who,* words linked to American culture	• Thinking about visiting people and gap-filling words in the song • Quiz on American culture	• Adding new verses to the song • Writing a quiz about a country
2.8 The animals went in two by two	8–10	animals and animal categories, rhyming words	• Matching rhyming sentences • Classifying animals onto a 'Tree of Life'	• Making a 'Tree of Life' poster • Designing a luxury ark
2.9 Jingle bells	8–10	seasonal activities and weather, 'Christmas' words, instructions	• Choosing correct words in the song • Making a pop-up Christmas card	• Making a class 'seasons' poster • Making new words from 'Christmastime'
2.10 Michael Finnegan	8–10	irregular past tenses, prepositions, opposites, board game instructions	• Ordering lines from the song • Matching opposites • 'Michael Finnegan' board game	• Singing the song faster and faster • Simon Says 'opposites'
2.11 Row, row, row your boat	8–10	things by a river, *If you see … , don't forget to … ,* action and 'noise' verbs, the water cycle	• Visualising things by a river • Gap-filling words of the song • Understanding the water cycle	• Creating a similar song about a car • Project on using and saving water
2.12 Oranges and lemons	8–10	shopping vocabulary and phrases, *When will … ?*	• Matching the bells and what they say • 'Oranges and lemons' playground game • Playing a shopping game	• Poster advertising an ideal shop • Researching what pupils' town looked like in the old days

Level 3	Age	Language covered	Worksheet activities	Follow-up activities
3.1 In the Quartermaster's store	10–12	animals and rhyming words, places in the town, giving directions	• Matching the animals and what they are doing in the song • Reading and following directions on a map	• Writing a new version of the song with pupils' names • Making a map of the local area
3.2 The house that Jack built	10–12	animals and people on a farm, people who build houses, action verbs, relative clauses	• Gap-filling the chant and chanting • Reading about people who build houses	• Creating a chant about the class • Designing an ideal home
3.3 On top of spaghetti	10–12	food and drink, rhyming words, restaurant language	• Tracking the meatball's experiences • Creating a menu and acting out a restaurant role-play	• Categorising foods into the different groups: meat, cereals, fruit, vegetables, and dairy • Project on food in different countries
3.4 Land of the silver birch	10–12	Canadian nature and animals	• Gap-filling the song • Making a totem pole with Canadian animal totems	• Creating a poster about an area of natural beauty • Creating a totem pole for animals from pupils' country
3.5 London Bridge is falling down	10–12	natural materials, big numbers, years and decimal numbers, superlatives, question word questions	• Learning about materials and their properties • Completing a factfile on four famous bridges	• Poster project on what different objects are made of • Researching a famous bridge or monument
3.6 The green grass grew all around	10–12	trees and nature, 'environment' vocabulary	• Labelling a 'nature' picture • Learning about the importance of trees	• Project on what comes from trees • Creating a questionnaire about helping the environment

Level 3	Age	Language covered	Worksheet activities	Follow-up activities
3.7 As I was going to St Ives	10–12	riddles and puzzles	• Understanding riddles • Solving a puzzle	• Telling jokes and riddles • Playing 'Twenty questions'
3.8 The twelve days of Christmas	10–12	ordinal numbers, dates, 'presents' in the song, truffle recipe ingredients and cooking instructions	• Matching song words and pictures • Making a Christmas truffles recipe	• Researching important dates round the world • Making Christmas truffles
3.9 When I first came to this land	10–12	rhyming words, family and farm vocabulary	• Introducing the pioneer and his story • Playing a 'Pioneer' game	• Making a 'pioneer homestead' poster • Researching farms in pupils' country
3.10 There's a hole in my bucket	10–12	things needed to mend a bucket, *to* for purpose, *too* + adjective, things to take on a camping trip	• Matching the problems with the bucket to the solutions • Planning a camping trip	• Finding uses for everyday objects • Snap
3.11 The Owl and the Pussycat	10–12	words of a nonsense poem, following origami instructions *fold, crease*, etc.	• Correcting mistakes in the story • Making an origami boat	• Researching poems by Edward Lear • Retelling the story
3.12 Waltzing Matilda	10–12	Australian English words, storytelling	• Matching Australian and British English words • Ordering the story of the song	• Creating a list of common slang words or different words in UK, American and Australian English • Acting out the story from the song

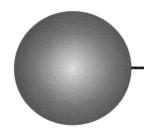

Introduction

What is *Primary Music Box?*

Primary Music Box is a multi-level, photocopiable resource book based around a collection of 36 traditional songs and rhymes. It has been designed to provide teachers with ready-to-use materials, thus minimising preparation time. It is intended for use with primary level English classes of 6 to 12 years old.

What does *Primary Music Box* aim to do?

Throughout history, and indeed long before the written word, songs have been used to amuse children, pass on moral and cultural messages, and simply to create a feeling of warmth and belonging between community members.

From a language teacher's perspective, singing together allows pupils to practise and perfect rhythms and intonation, and memorise language almost effortlessly, in a fun, stress-free and non-competitive atmosphere.

Traditional songs have an added benefit of introducing some aspects of native culture in an enjoyable and natural way.

So, the aims of *Primary Music* Box are threefold. Firstly, to provide a set of highly enjoyable activities for pupils and teacher alike; secondly, to practise grammar and vocabulary, which will be genuinely useful for all pupils across the primary age range and, finally, to offer an opportunity for pupils to explore the culture or topic behind these songs and rhymes.

What does *Primary Music Box* contain?

• Components

– *Primary Music Box* Resource Book with full teacher's notes and lesson plans, photocopiable worksheets and song lyrics

– *Primary Music Box* CD containing recordings of all 36 songs

• Levels

Primary Music Box is organised into three levels with 12 songs at each level. Although, as the songs are traditional, some of the vocabulary and structures fall outside the recommended word and structure lists for Cambridge Young Learners *Starters*, *Movers* and *Flyers* tests, the songs have been chosen, (and in some cases, slightly adapted), and the lessons adapted to suit the language level and conceptual abilities of pupils in the following groups:

Level 1: suitable for pupils aged 6 to 8 who are starting their English studies as beginners. The first half of Level 1 has been designed not to include any reading activities.

Level 2: suitable for pupils aged 7 to 10 who are at an elementary level.

Level 3: suitable for pupils aged 10 to 12 who are at pre-intermediate level.

These levels are intended as a guide only. You should use your own judgement as to whether a particular song will work well with your class. Pupils do not need to understand every single word in order to fully enjoy and benefit from the activities based around a song, although the lesson plans, illustrations and worksheets have been designed to give as full support to the comprehension of the songs as possible.

• Ready-to-use materials

Each level of *Primary Music Box* contains 12 easy-to-use lesson plans. Each lesson plan is based around one song and is accompanied by two photocopiable worksheets.

– Worksheet 1 exploits the language of the song itself. Fun activities and games are designed to help pupils with staged comprehension of the song and to teach or check vocabulary.

– Worksheet 2 offers an extension to the topic of the song, usually through a project or creative activity. These worksheets often offer an opportunity for cross-curricular teaching.

• Resource bank

Ideas are given in the teacher's notes for two Follow-up activities at the end of each lesson. A fuller description of how to set up these and other activities referred to in the lesson plans is included in the Resource bank (p.13).

The Resource bank also provides generic ideas for using songs in the classroom.

• Song lyrics

A complete set of song lyrics is provided (p.126). These are mainly intended for the teacher, although they can be photocopied and given out to the pupils, where appropriate.

If the song words are given out, we recommend that you do so after pupils have had a chance to complete worksheet 1, which has been designed to introduce the song meaning and part or all of the text in a more graded way.

If appropriate, the song lyrics can be used to create further activities – for example, cutting up the song for pupils to put in the correct order, or creating additional gap-fills by whiting out some of the text. Pupils could also be encouraged to decorate their lyric sheets and take them home to teach the song to their family.

How can I use *Primary Music Box* in the classroom?

• Choosing a song

The traditional songs in *Primary Music Box* were not specifically written or designed to teach or practise English. Rather, they are songs that native speaker children of the same age will be singing with their parents and friends on school trips or camping holidays or at a party.

Nevertheless, many of the songs naturally lend themselves to the practice of a specific grammar point or lexical set. A breakdown of the language and themes covered in each song is provided at the top of each page of teacher's notes under Language Focus and in the Map of the Book (p. 3).

It is not necessary to follow the songs in *Primary Music Box* in the order that they appear in the book. Use your judgement to choose the songs that fit in best with language or other topics that you are teaching in your curriculum.

• Following the teacher's notes

The teacher's notes for each song include a summary of language, target age group, timings for each stage and materials needed, together with a clearly staged lesson plan, and suggestions for Follow-up activities.

The notes list how many copies of each worksheet you need for your class, together with any additional materials or preparation that is needed. This additional preparation has been kept to a minimum. You will also need a copy of the song recording for each lesson.

Each lesson is divided into three steps, each of which can be completed in roughly 20 to 30 minutes. Depending on the time available, you can choose to do all three steps together in a single lesson, or split them over three separate lessons.

Step 1 introduces the theme of the song and the key language. In this step, pupils will listen to the song for the first time whilst completing a simple task, such as doing actions or identifying words and the order of the song but will not be asked to sing.

Step 2 is where the song is sung and practised in full and further comprehension and extension work takes place.

In *Step 3*, the theme, grammar and/or vocabulary of the song is reinforced and extended through a project or creative activity.

The suggested timing for each step is included in the teacher's notes. This is intended only as a guide. Pupils' capacity to do any particular lesson or activity will depend on their level of English and on their conceptual awareness.

The material is designed so that, if done in a single lesson, it contains a good balance of active and more calming, desk-based activities.

If you choose to split the material over three lessons, make sure that pupils write their names on any worksheets they use. Collect them in and keep them safely for the following lesson.

Also bear in mind that pupils will need reminding of the song and activities in the previous step, before progressing onto the step for that day. Suggestions for doing this are included at the start of each step in the lesson plans.

The phrase *If necessary* in the lesson plans suggests that you could skip this introductory part of a step if your pupils are doing two consecutive steps in one lesson.

Sometimes optional activities are suggested in the lesson plan. These are indicated in brackets.

The Follow-up activities suggested in the teacher's notes can either be done as part of the same lesson, or used as the basis of a separate extension lesson.

Further guidance on how to set up any of the activities suggested in the lesson plans is provided in the Resource bank (p. 13).

• Classroom management

While singing together is generally a pleasurable experience, it can give rise to some particular classroom management issues. Suggestions are given below for dealing with these:

– Noise. Pupils can get very enthusiastic with their singing. If the class gets too noisy, try getting pupils to sing softly or in a whisper on purpose. This is fun and often solves the problem. Teaching a signal to *Be quiet* or *Stop singing* also helps.

– Movement. Some of the songs feature actions which require pupils to move around the classroom. While they can perform many of the actions at their desks, some songs will ask them to stand up or come to the front of the class. Take care to organise these movements systematically. Set clear rules from the outset that pupils must move calmly when doing these activities. If any activity starts to get out of hand, pupils can be sent back to their desks immediately. If the rules are respected, allowing pupils to move while they sing will increase both their enjoyment of the song and the learning benefits.

– Embarrassment. Some pupils may find singing aloud embarrassing if they are not confident of their singing voices. It is up to the teacher to take the lead and show them that there is nothing to worry about. Having the recording to sing along to will also help everybody keep in tune.

• Use of English and L1

We recommend that the lessons are taught in English as far as possible. Suggested English phrasing is provided in the lesson plans to facilitate this.

However, there are also times when use of the mother tongue provides a useful classroom management tool. These may include times when you want pupils to contribute their ideas or opinions, especially when discussing an extension of a topic or simply as a quick check of understanding.

Use your judgement to decide when using the L1 is appropriate. You could control this by teaching pupils to say the phrase *May I speak (L1)?* before this is allowed.

What activities does Primary Music Box provide?

Primary Music Box provides a wealth of activities specifically designed to meet the needs of young learners. The main types of activities are as follows:

• Warmers

These are included at the beginning of each lesson step. They are designed to motivate pupils and get them involved in that stage of the lesson and also, in Steps 2 and 3, remind them of what has gone before.

• Speaking activities

The teacher's notes in *Primary Music Box* include a variety of speaking activities. These include pair dictations, quizzes, acting out and retelling stories, making up rhymes, doing surveys and completing information-gap activities. A more detailed description of the individual activities is included in the lesson plans and in the Resource bank.

• Drama

Many lesson plans in *Primary Music Box* offer pupils an opportunity to act things out. When pupils are acting out a role-play, make sure pupils respect each other's turns and are quiet, so that everyone can see and hear.

• Games

Games are an extremely motivating way for pupils to learn and practise new language. Games in *Primary Music Box* include guessing games, card games, word games and board games.

• TPR and mime

Total Physical Response (TPR) and mime improve comprehension and memory by increasing pupils' active involvement in listening. Many of the songs in *Primary Music Box* have actions and movements for pupils to learn and do as they sing the song. These include movements that native speakers will traditionally learn and do when singing these songs at home or in the playground.

• Craft activities

Many of the worksheets contain an element of cutting out or construction. These activities are very motivating for pupils and help with their understanding of a topic.

Make sure that pupils always have access to all the materials they will need, as described in the teacher's notes (e.g. scissors, sticky tape, glue, pencils, paper or card). It is also useful to teach pupils the names of these objects and 'craft' verbs such as *cut*, *stick* or *fold*.

Where possible, make an example of the completed craft item to show pupils. This will motivate them and also indicate any areas where they may need extra help.

Display pupils' creations in the classroom if possible or encourage them to take them home to show their parents.

• Listening activities

Each song in *Primary Music Box* provides a natural listening activity. Pupils are encouraged to develop different listening skills, including listening for general meaning or listening for specific information. Each Worksheet 1 provides an active task to engage pupils' listening skills, such as: listen and draw, listen and order a sequence, listen and match, listen and complete a sentence, etc.

• Reading activities

Reading activities are included from song 7 at Level 1. Pupils are exposed to a wide variety of reading texts and activities. These include simpler song-specific activities, such as read and match or gap-fill, as well as stories, information texts and instructions to follow.

• Writing activities

Pupils are encouraged to start writing from the start of Level 2. This is usually in the form of graded activities, such as completing a gap-fill or copying words and sentences into the appropriate place on the worksheet. The Follow-up activities suggested include many ideas for freer writing activities.

• Cross-curricular activities

The content of some of the songs in *Primary Music Box* lends itself naturally to extension into cross-curricular topic work. Many of the second worksheets for each song are designed to exploit this. Examples of topics covered include transport, musical instruments, farm and wild animals, North America, the water cycle, the environment, food and food hygiene, materials and people involved in a building project.

• Christmas activities

Each level of *Primary Music Box* includes one song that can be used at Christmastime. As well as learning a traditional Christmas song, pupils will make something that they can take home and give to their family as a present.

Primary Music Box

Resource bank

This Resource bank contains:

- ideas for exploiting songs generally
- background information for some of the songs and activities in *Primary Music Box*
- instructions for some of the Follow-up activities suggested in the teacher's notes

Ideas for exploiting songs

There are many ways of exploiting songs, many of which are suggested in the specific notes for each song in *Primary Music Box*. They are listed here for you to try out on other songs with your pupils.

• Repetition

Play the song as often as necessary, and sing songs again in subsequent lessons, if appropriate. Repetition is one of the best ways of learning and remembering. Learning by rote has been much criticised but it is recognised that repeated exposure to vocabulary items is a vital aspect of learning, and singing together is a valuable means of doing this in a fun way.

• Singing rounds

Many songs lend themselves to being sung in rounds, for example, song 2.2 (Kookaburra). Divide the class into four groups. Group 1 starts singing the song alone. As Group 1 continues with the second line, Group 2 starts singing from the beginning. As Group 1 continues with the third line, Group 3 starts from the beginning. And finally as Group 1 starts singing the last line, Group 4 starts singing from the beginning. The groups can stop after singing the song once, or repeat the verse again. Some beautiful harmonies can be produced in this way.

• Fast/Slow/Funny

It is great fun to get the pupils to sing the song very quickly, or very slowly, or in a funny voice, for example, very deep or very high. They can also sing with particular emotions, such as happiness, sadness, anger or shyness. This activity is best used when pupils are thoroughly familiar with the song and its melody, and can concentrate on the special effect they are trying to achieve.

• Cutting the music/volume

As pupils are singing along with the recording, pause the music suddenly to see if they sing the next word or phrase correctly. Start the music again to check.

Alternatively, reduce the volume without stopping the music to hear how the pupils sound and if they are following the song properly. This activity is fun because the pupils don't know when you will put them in the spotlight. If you turn the sound down just before a word or phrase they know well, you will find they proudly sing along with lots of enthusiasm.

• Clapping

The rhythm of a song, and of the English language, can usefully be practised through clapping along. An example of this can be found in song 1.7 (Bingo). Another advantage of this activity is that it is kinaesthetic (i.e. physical), but pupils don't have to leave their seats to do it.

Group 1 sing	Line 1	Line 2	Line 3	Line 4			
Group 2 sing		Line 1	Line 2	Line 3	Line 4		
Group 3 sing			Line 1	Line 2	Line 3	Line 4	
Group 4 sing				Line 1	Line 2	Line 3	Line 4

• Doing actions to the songs

Many of the songs in *Primary Music Box* feature traditional actions that are practised by native speakers as they sing the songs themselves. Actions can be invented for many of the other songs, too. Acting out songs is a marvellous technique. Not only are the pupils totally involved in the activity, they are also concentrating on the actions and forgetting they are in an English lesson. In this way, the words come naturally and are remembered more profoundly.

• Singing in groups

Where there are different roles, for example, Henry and Liza in song 3.10 (There's a hole in my bucket), parts of the song can be sung by different pupils or groups. Alternate lines can be assigned to two halves of the class or different verses to the different groups and the chorus to everyone. More confident pupils can be also assigned individual lines to sing as a solo.

• Using props

Pupils can demonstrate their understanding of the song by holding up a certain picture or item at the appropriate time as they listen. This physical activity, involving both listening and choosing, based on what they hear, strongly reinforces the learning process and can be exploited wherever a song includes strong visual images.

• Adding new verses or adapting the song

Many of the songs in *Primary Music Box* are suitable for adding new verses or adapting to include information about people in the class. For example, new musical instruments can be added to song 1.5 (The music man), new body parts to song 2.1 (The Hokey Cokey), different answers to song 2.6 (I found a peanut) or new animals to song 2.8 (The animals went in two by two). Suggestions are also made for songs 1.7 (Bingo), 1.11 (Here we go round the mulberry bush), 2.7 (She'll be coming round the mountain), 2.11 (Row, row, row your boat) and 3.1 (In the Quartermaster's store). This should usually be done after the other activities in the lesson have been completed, and could be assigned to prepare as homework or done in a later lesson.

• Recording your pupils

Allowing your pupils to hear themselves or see themselves performing on film gives a tremendous boost to their enthusiasm. It is also a valuable teaching aid, as pupils will be able to gauge their progress, as well as identify things they have to work on, in a way they can't when they are actually singing. If appropriate, the film can also be shown to friends and family.

• Putting on a show

Pupils can be given the opportunity to show how well they can sing in English by organising a show for the school or parents during a special event, such as an open day. This can be a simple group recital of the songs they know, or an elaborate acting out of stories, along with costumes, actions and different pupils singing different lines.

Background notes to some of the songs

• Song 2.8 (The animals went in two by two) Step 1 the story of the Ark

In many cultures, there are stories of a great flood. They relate where the water came from and what happened to the people and animals on the earth. In the story of Noah's Ark, Noah is warned that there will be a flood and starts to build a large boat, which can house two of each animal and himself and his family. When the rain begins, they all enter the Ark and stay there for 40 days and 40 nights. The rest of the world is destroyed but, eventually, dry land reappears and they are saved.

• Song 2.12 (Oranges and lemons) Step 2 playground game

Pupils stand in two lines facing each other. Each pupil joins hands with the pupil facing them and they all hold up their arms to form a tunnel. Everyone starts to sing the song. The pair of pupils at the top of the line then walk down through the tunnel and stand up again at the far end, rejoining the tunnel with their arms in the air. This continues until the last two lines of the song. For these lines, pupils move their hands up and down as they sing, trapping the pupils walking through and letting them go. The pupils caught in the trap when they sing *The last man's dead* are out of the game.

• Song 2.12 (Oranges and lemons) Step 3 shopping dialogue

Shopkeeper: *Hello, how can I help you?*

Customer: *I'd like some apples, please.*

Shopkeeper: *How many would you like?*

Customer: *Three, please.*

Shopkeeper: *Here you are. That's £1.20 please.*

Customer: *Here you are.*

Shopkeeper: *Thank you. Bye.*

Follow-up activities

Each set of teacher's notes in *Primary Music Box* includes two additional Follow-up activities. Further explanation of how to set up and exploit these activity types is given here.

• Bingo

(Songs: 1.1 Ten in the bed, 1.3 Hickory dickory dock)

For numbers Bingo in Song 1.1 (Ten in the bed), ask pupils to choose four numbers from 1 to 10 and write them down on a piece of paper. Read out the numbers in a jumbled order. When pupils hear a number they have written down, they cross it out. The first pupil to cross out all four numbers calls out *Bingo!*

The same game can be played with larger numbers or with any other vocabulary set e.g. sets of clock faces or times for song 1.3 (Hickory dickory dock).

• Snap

(Songs: 1.2 The wheels on the bus, 1.12 There was a princess long ago, 3.10 There's a hole in my bucket)

Pupils work in pairs. They deal out the cards equally. Pupils then take turns to place a card from their pack face up on top of a central pile. If the card they are placing matches the one already at the top of the pile, either pupil can call out *Snap!* The first player to call out *Snap!* wins the pile of cards on the table. The player who ends up with all the cards is the winner.

• Pelmanism

(Songs: 1.2 The wheels on the bus, 1.3 Hickory dickory dock)

This game can be played in pairs or groups of three or four. Pupils need two sets of cards e.g. a set of clock faces and a set of equivalent clock times. They shuffle the two sets of cards and lay them out in two sections, face down on the table. Pupils then take turns to try to find matching pairs. One pupil turns up a card from each section. If the cards match, he/she keeps the pair and has another turn. If they don't, he/she turns the cards face down again in the same position and another pupil has a turn. As the game goes on, pupils will start to remember where certain cards are, and will find matching pairs by using their memory.

• Doing a picture dictation

(Songs: 1.1 Ten in the bed, 1.4 Dingle, dangle scarecrow, 1.6 We wish you a Merry Christmas, 1.10 There was an old lady)

The teacher can do the dictation for the pupils or pupils can work in pairs. One dictates/describes a picture for the other pupil to draw. For example, the Christmas dictation for song 1.6 could be: *There is a big Christmas tree. I can see four presents. The presents are red, yellow, green and blue. I can see Father Christmas!* If a pupil is describing an existing picture, their partner should not be able to see it while they are drawing. They can then compare pictures at the end.

• Making a word snake

(Song: 1.7 Bingo)

Pupils use cut-up letters to make a chain (or snake) of words, each of which begins with the last letter of the previous word. These can be words from one particular lexical set (birdogiraffelephanturtlemu) or whatever words they have the letters to form (legardenoselephantrumpetrainight). If pupils work in two groups, the two groups can then try to find the words that are in the other's word snake.

• Hangman

(Song: 1.7 Bingo)

One pupil secretly chooses a word, checks the spelling with the teacher and then writes dashes on the board, one for each letter in the word. Other pupils take turns to guess what letters are in the word. If a pupil guesses a letter correctly, all the examples of that letter must be filled in above the dashes. If a letter is not in the word, the pupil writes it at the bottom of the board, and draws one line of a hangman's scaffold or one part of the body hanging from it. A typically completed scaffold would look like the diagram below. This gives the class ten chances to guess the word. If someone calls out the correct word before the scaffold is complete, they are the winner and can choose the next word. If no one guesses before the scaffold is complete, the original pupil is the winner.

CAT

B M W O L F E N S

• Acting out or retelling a fairy tale or story

(Songs: 1.12 There was a princess long ago, 3.11 The Owl and the Pussycat, 3.12 Waltzing Matilda)

Ask the class to choose a fairy tale or story they know well. Start by telling a short version of the story together. Write key words on the board. For a simple acting out of the story, ask individual pupils to mime the characters in the story as you read it out again.

For a more challenging activity, divide pupils into groups and allocate each pupil in the group a role. Allow pupils some time to come up with some dialogue for each role. They write this down. Help as necessary and give them time to practise. Groups then perform their versions of the story in front of the class.

• Simon Says

(Songs: 2.1 The Hokey Cokey, 2.10 Michael Finnegan)

This is an instructions game. Call out instructions, using the format *Simon says (touch your toes)*. Pupils have to obey your instructions. If you call out an instruction without saying *Simon says* first (e.g. *Touch your toes!*), pupils shouldn't obey the instruction and should stand still. Any pupil who doesn't follow these rules is out of the game. The winner is the last player in the game. Pupils can also play this game in pairs or small groups. In the Michael Finnegan version, the teacher calls out an instruction and pupils have to do the opposite e.g. *Simon says stand on your right leg* (pupils stand on their left leg).

• Exploring the senses

(Song: 2.1 The Hokey Cokey)

Elicit or teach the sense verbs: *I see with my eyes, I hear with my ears, I smell with my nose, I taste with my mouth, I touch with my hands.* Then do some simple activities in class for pupils to explore the senses. Ask *What can you see in the classroom?* Pupils look. Ask pupils to shut their eyes and ask *What can you hear?* Make sounds as necessary for pupils to guess. With their eyes still shut you can ask pupils to smell or feel things and guess what they are e.g. smell or feel a pencil. You could also bring things to class for pupils to taste, but be aware of any food allergies. Make a big paper tongue, give pupils different things that are e.g. sweet, salty, bitter, sour, and get them to draw pictures of the foods to stick on the appropriate place on the tongue.

• Guess the ... /Twenty questions

(Songs: 1.8 Old Macdonald, 2.2 Kookaburra, 3.7 As I was going to St Ives)

This game can be played in pairs, small groups or the whole class and with any vocabulary set. Here we suggest playing it with zoo animals. One pupil secretly chooses an animal. The other has to guess by asking questions where the answer can only be *Yes* or *No.* For example, *Is it big? Can it swim? Has it got two legs? Is it a reptile?* They are allowed to ask a maximum of 20 questions. If they guess the animal within these 20 questions, they score a point. If not, the pupil who has chosen the animal scores a point.

• Doing a project

(Songs: 2.3 This old man, 2.4 We've got the whole world in our hands, 2.11 Row, row, row your boat, 3.3 On top of spaghetti, 3.5 London Bridge is falling down, 3.6 The green grass grew all around)

Many of the songs in *Primary Music Box* lend themselves to follow-up projects. These suggestions are based on the one on how to look after pets, for Song 2.3 (This old man).

Pupils work in pairs or small groups. They choose a pet they have or would like to have. Explain that they are going to find out information first, and take notes, then choose some of the information to write up and present.

If they already own that pet, they can start by writing down all the things they already know about looking after it. Then they write a list of questions to ask their parent, or someone else who owns that pet e.g. *What does it eat? Where does it sleep?* Encourage pupils to look in the school library for information about their chosen animal. They can also search for information on the Internet. When they have the information they need, encourage them to choose approximately six facts to write up. These should include what the animal eats and drinks, any special equipment needed, where it sleeps and possible problems with the animal. Pupils can illustrate their projects with photos or drawings of the animals and the whole thing can be mounted and displayed on the classroom wall.

• Keeping a recycling diary

(Song: 2.4 We've got the whole world in our hands)

Pupils keep a record of the rubbish they recycle at home over two days. Prepare in class by showing pupils how to make a table, listing the days and the type of rubbish that can be recycled:

Recycled	(Saturday)	(Sunday)
plastic		
paper		
glass		
clothes		
food		
metal		

They take this home and record the number of each item that they put out for recycling. If they don't recycle a particular type of item, they enter an x in the box. They then bring the completed table back to class for discussion.

• Putting on a talent show

(Song: 2.5 Do your ears hang low?)

Pupils work individually or in groups. If in groups, each group thinks of something they can do together e.g. an exercise routine, touching their toes, singing a song, doing a dance, saying a poem, etc. The groups then take turns to perform their talent to the rest of the class. You could make the show more special by making a 'running order' and being or appointing a master of ceremonies to introduce each 'act'.

• Making a poster

(Songs: 1.2 The wheels on the bus, 1.8 Old Macdonald had a farm, 1.9 If you're happy and you know it, 2.6 I found a peanut, 2.8 The animals went in two by two, 2.9 Jingle bells, 2.12 Oranges and lemons, 3.4 Land of the silver birch, 3.5 London Bridge is falling down, 3.9 When I first came to this land)

Many of the songs in *Primary Music Box* lend themselves to the activity of making a class poster. The one suggested below is for the food safety poster in song 2.6 (I found a peanut).

Discuss some Dos and Don'ts of food hygiene with the class e.g. *Wash your hands before eating. Always wash or peel fruit and vegetables. Eat food from a plate. Don't eat food* from the floor. *Keep food in a fridge. Don't leave food in the sun,* etc. Pupils can then take some of these ideas to make a food safety poster.

Take a big piece of paper and draw a line to divide it into two halves. Label one of these *Do* and the other *Don't.*

Pupils draw pictures and write sentences to stick onto the poster. They can work on these individually or in pairs or small groups. Make sure each pupil or group of pupils is working on a different picture. When they have finished, add their drawings to the poster paper in the correct column.

• Writing a quiz

(Song: 2.7 She'll be coming round the mountain)

Pupils work in small groups. They choose a country they are interested in. Explain that they are going to find out about their chosen country first and take notes. Then they are going to write some questions about it for the rest of the class to answer. They can start by writing down things they already know about their chosen country. They then write a list of questions or topic areas e.g. food, clothes, they would like to find out about. They find out the answers by asking their parents or other adults, by looking in books in the school library and by researching on the Internet. When they have enough information, ask them to write five questions. Swap the quizzes around, and ask the class to answer each other's.

• Designing a luxury ark

(Song: 2.8 The animals went in two by two)

Pupils work in small groups. Ask them to imagine what the Ark from the song might look like inside. Then ask them to imagine the Ark is a luxurious five-star hotel for the animals. What kind of things might it contain? Encourage them to be as imaginative as possible e.g. swimming pool, restaurant, race track for exercise, etc. Then distribute paper and pencils and ask pupils to design a luxury ark, using all their ideas. Display the finished results around the classroom.

• Doing research

(Songs: 2.12 Oranges and lemons, 3.5 London Bridge is falling down, 3.8 The twelve days of Christmas, 3.9 When I first came to this land, 3.11 The Owl and the Pussycat)

Many of the songs lend themselves to pupils doing further research on the topic. For example, in song 2.12, pupils are encouraged to find out what their street or town looked like in the old days. It is always a good idea to prepare pupils by getting them to agree on a limited number of things to find out about and focusing their research on those areas. Family members, neighbours, local libraries and information centres are the best source of information for this kind of research. You are also likely to find pictures by searching on the Internet. If it's not possible to find pictures to bring to class, arrange a class trip to the local library. Or pupils can do sketches of the oldest buildings in their street, town or country. Information that pupils discover can then be put together as a class poster or project.

• Writing a questionnaire about the environment

(Song: 3.6 The green grass grew all around)

Pupils work together as a class. Choose some simple ideas about helping the environment to discuss with the class e.g. pollution, rubbish and recycling and saving energy. Ask questions about each topic to get pupils thinking about how we are damaging the environment and what we can do to help. Keep the questions as conceptually simple as possible e.g. *What causes traffic pollution?* (cars, planes, buses, etc.) *What can we do to cause less traffic pollution?* (walk, cycle, use buses more than cars, etc.) *How much of our rubbish can we recycle? What uses energy?* (electricity, gas, fuel for cars, etc.) *How can we save energy?* (Turn lights off, turn electricity off when not using it, wash clothes at lower temperatures, etc.)

When you have discussed ideas with the class, tell them you are going to make a questionnaire together to find out what their parents and friends are doing for the environment. Elicit some questions from them and write them on the board e.g. *Do you travel by car or by bus? When you go out of a room, do you switch the light off? How do you travel on holiday? Where do you go? What rubbish do you recycle?* Limit the questionnaire to about six to ten questions. Pupils then copy the questions down and take the questionnaires home to ask their parents and neighbours.

• Making Christmas truffles

(Song: 3.8 The twelve days of Christmas)

If you have access to a kitchen, try making the Christmas truffles recipe with your class. You can either do this by demonstrating making them yourself, and asking individual pupils to help with certain tasks, or dividing the class into groups to make them themselves. Make sure you have all the ingredients and utensils you will need. If you only have one set of utensils, but still want pupils to work in groups, assign each group one task. For example, group 1 measures out the ingredients, group 2 adds the ingredients to the bowl and stirs them together, group 3 shapes the ingredients into small balls, group 4 rolls the balls in chocolate strands and puts them into cake cases.

Ten in the bed

numbers *1–10*
bedroom furniture
personal possessions
prepositions of place *in, on, in front of, between, next to, behind, under*

LEVEL 1

AGE RANGE 6–7

TIME
Step 1: 30 minutes
Step 2: 20 minutes
Step 3: 15 minutes

MATERIALS

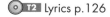 Lyrics p.126

Step 1
Worksheet 1 for each pair of pupils, sticky tape and scissors, colouring pencils, a completed set of ten finger puppets for yourself, large book

Step 2
Your own and pupils' completed finger puppets

Step 3
Worksheet 2 for each pupil plus 1 x A3 copy, colouring pencils

FOLLOW-UP ACTIVITIES

Class play numbers Bingo (p.14)

Pupils draw their own bedroom or design their ideal bedroom

Step 1 Reviewing numbers *1–10* forwards and backwards, making finger puppets, listening to and acting out the song

Step 2 Learning and singing the song with actions, reviewing/learning prepositions of place

Step 3 Reviewing/Learning items of bedroom furniture, picture dictation

Step 1

1 Put a set of finger puppets on your hands. Say *Look at my fingers and listen.* Count up to ten, wiggling the correct number of fingers for each number you say.

2 Say *Now count with me.* Drill the numbers using the puppets.

3 Put pupils into pairs. Give each pair one copy of worksheet 1, scissors, sticky tape and colouring pencils. Say *Where are the children?* Establish that they're in a big bed. Show pupils how to cut out figures – five each – colour them, then stick them to make puppets.

4 Pupil pairs wear five puppets each. Call out different numbers. In their pairs, pupils put up the correct number of fingers.

5 With your own puppets, demonstrate counting backwards from ten to zero and drill the sequence. Say different numbers and say *What comes next?*

6 Using a large book as a bed, place your ten puppets tightly together on it with the little one 'squashed' in the middle. Establish that the little one can't 'roll over'.

7 Say *But listen to this song.* Play the song. Each time 'one falls out', knock one puppet off. Continue until only the 'little one' is left and yawns *Goodnight.* Repeat the song for pupils to act out with their own puppets.

Step 2

1 If necessary, remind pupils of the song by saying *Let's play Ten in the bed.* Get pupils to act it out with their puppets while they listen.

2 Drill the first two verses. Then get pupils to sing along while acting the song out with their puppets.

3 Put your little puppet on the table and say *Where's the little one?* Elicit *on the table.* Then draw an open box and chair on the board. Stick the puppet in different places to elicit/teach the prepositions of place *in, on, in front of, between, next to, behind, under.*

4 As practice, give pupils instructions to place one or a number of their finger puppets in different places e.g. *Put three children between two pencils / behind a book / under the chair / on your fingers,* etc. Pupils then practise in pairs.

Step 3

1 Stick the A3 copy of worksheet 2 on the board. Say *What's this?* Elicit/Teach *a bedroom.*

2 Drill the items round the picture *armchair, bookcase, toy box, clock, computer, lamp, table, mat, picture, radio.*

3 Put pupils into pairs. Give each pair one copy of worksheet 2. Repeat the words in random order. Get pupils to point to the relevant picture.

4 Say *Look. Put the table next to the bed.* Draw a line on your A3 picture to show where to put the table. Get pupils to come and draw lines as you give instructions for all the objects, using different prepositions of place.

5 Give each pupil worksheet 2. Give different instructions and make a note of them. Pupils draw lines in pencil on their worksheets.

6 Pupils check their worksheets in pairs. Help with mistakes.

7 Pupils can finish the lesson by either colouring in the pictures or rubbing out the lines and dictating different instructions to their partner. (p.15)

Cut out and make the finger puppets. Listen and act out the song.

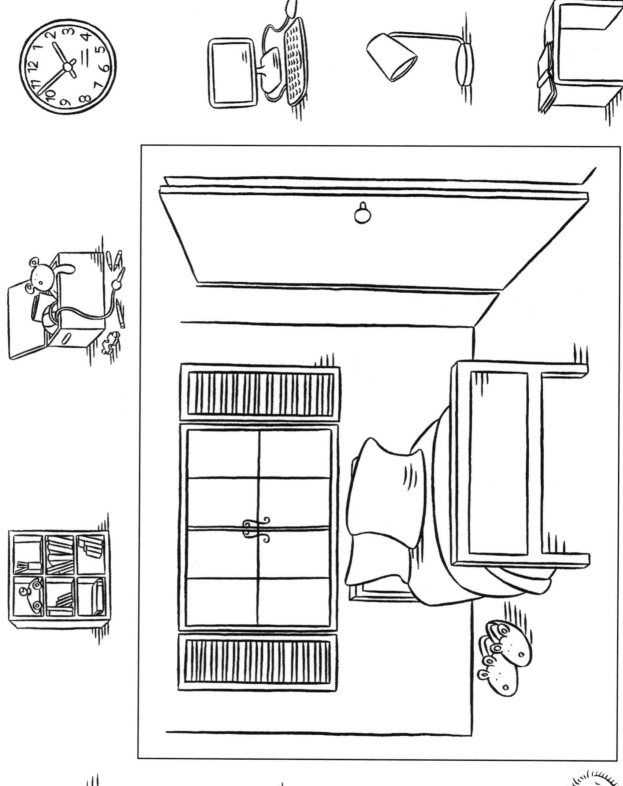

  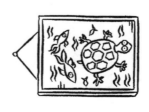 

 Primary Music Box © Cambridge University Press 2010

Listen and draw lines.

The wheels on the bus

1.2

LANGUAGE FOCUS
transport
sounds on a bus
*Do you go by ...?, Yes I do,
No I don't*

LEVEL 1

AGE RANGE 6–8

TIME
Step 1: 20 minutes
Step 2: 20 minutes
Step 3: 20 minutes

MATERIALS
T3 Lyrics p.126

Step 1
Flashcards of blown-up
pictures of bus 'features' from
worksheet 1

Step 2
Flashcards of blown-up
pictures of 'features' and
'actions' from worksheet 1,
worksheet 1 for each pupil,
scissors

Step 3
Worksheet 2 for each pupil
plus 1 x A3 copy

**FOLLOW-UP
ACTIVITIES**
Class play Snap or Pelmanism
with cut-out cards from
worksheet 1 (p.15)

Pupils create posters of
different types of transport for
road, sea and air (p.16)

Step 1 Learning the features of the bus, listening to and acting out the song
Step 2 Learning the song and singing it with actions
Step 3 Class survey on types of transport used by pupils

Step 1

1 Draw a large bus outline on the board, showing the front and side. Say *What's this?* (*a bus*). Using flashcards of the six 'features' of the bus, elicit/teach *wheels, wipers, money, mums, dads* and *bell*. Drill *the wheels on the bus/the wipers on the bus*, etc. Stick the pictures on the bus in appropriate places.

2 Say *Now let's listen to a song about the bus. Put your hand up when you hear the words.* Play the recording. As the class identifies each feature, take the pictures off the bus and stick them on the board in the order of the song.

3 Say *Listen. The wheels on the bus go round and round.* Demonstrate as you are speaking by rolling your hands around each other. Say *Now you do that.* Continue down the list of actions until pupils are familiar with them all (see worksheet 1). (*swish* – move arms like wipers; *chink* – clench and shake hand as if holding money; *chatter* – open and close fingers and thumb like a mouth; *ssh* – put finger in front of mouth; *ding* – press a button.)

4 Say *Now let's listen to the song and do the actions.* As the song plays, point to the wheels, the wipers and so on, miming the actions. Pupils copy.

Step 2

1 If necessary, remove the 'features' pictures from the board. Give each pupil worksheet 1, to cut up themselves. Pupils order the features as in the song, then match them to the appropriate 'action' picture. Monitor.

2 Using the 'actions' flashcards, teach and drill phrases for the actions *go round and round / go swish, swish, swish / goes chink, chink, chink, go chatter, chatter, chatter, go ssh, ssh, ssh, goes ding, ding, ding,* etc.

3 Check by using the 'actions' cards randomly and saying *What do the mums do?* (*the mums on the bus go chatter, chatter, chatter,* etc.) (If time, pupils can use their own sets of cards to practise with each other.)

4 Say *Now let's sing the song and do the actions together.*

Step 3

1 Elicit what the song was about (*a bus*). Draw a plane on the board and say *What's this?* Drill *It's a plane.* Repeat with the other types of transport from worksheet 2 *car, lorry/truck, boat, train, motorbike, bike, bus.*

2 Get pupils to come to the board and draw different vehicles. The class guess what they are.

3 Stick the A3 copy of worksheet 2 on the board. Ask individual pupils *Do you go by bike/ motorbike?* etc. Teach *Yes I do / No I don't.* Each time a pupil says *Yes*, write their name above 'Me' and put a tick in the appropriate column. Give each pupil worksheet 2. Pupils tick for themselves as appropriate in the 'Me' row.

4 Divide pupils into groups of six to ten. Say *Now ask the people in your group the questions.* Pupils write all the names in the first column, ask everyone in the group *Do you go by bike/ car/plane?*, etc. and record the *Yes* answers with ticks.

5 Groups report back. *In our group, five people go by bus / one person goes by taxi,* etc.

Cut out the cards. Match the things on the bus to the actions.

The wheels on the bus 2

Ask your friends *Do you go by … ?* Write their names and tick (✔) for Yes.

Name	Name	Name	Name	Name	Name	Name	Name	Name	Me	

Hickory dickory dock

LANGUAGE FOCUS
numbers *1–12*
*o'clock, What time is it?,
It's ... ,
What time do you ... ?,
I ... at ... o'clock*
daily routines

LEVEL 1

AGE RANGE 6–7

TIME
Step 1: 15 minutes
Step 2: 30 minutes
Step 3: 30 minutes

MATERIALS
 **T4** Lyrics p.127

Step 1
A blown-up mouse from
worksheet 1 stuck to the top
of a pencil, a blown-up and
completed clock face with
hands from worksheet 1

Step 2
Worksheet 1 for each pupil,
(1 x A4 sheet of card for
each pupil, glue), scissors,
colouring pencils, brass pins
for attaching the clock hands
to the face, a hole punch,
sticky tape

Step 3
Worksheet 2 for each pupil
plus 1 x A3 copy, a blown-up
clock

**FOLLOW-UP
ACTIVITIES**
Pupils make a picture
timetable of their activities at
different times of day

Class play time Bingo or
Pelmanism with sets of clock
faces and times (p.14, 15)

Step 1	Learning/Reviewing clock hours, *It's ... o'clock* and *What time is it?*, listening to the song
Step 2	Making a clock face and mouse, asking for and telling the time, learning the song and singing it
Step 3	Class survey on asking and talking about daily routines

Step 1

1 Stick your blown-up clock on the board. Say *What's this?* (*a clock*). Move the hands to 1 o'clock. Say *What time is it?* (*It's 1 o'clock*). Repeat for *2 o'clock*, etc. up to 12. Drill each answer.

2 Elicit/Teach *What time is it, please?* Get pupils to come out and ask you for the time. Say different times e.g. *It's 6 o'clock* for each pupil to put the hands at the right time on the clock.

3 Set the clock at different times and get pupils to tell you the time.

4 Show the class your mouse. Say *What's this?* Say *Let's listen to a song about a mouse and a clock*. Play the first verse. Move the mouse up the clock, tap it once on the clock face and say '*bong*' for *The clock struck one* then move the mouse down the clock.

5 Play the whole song. Pupils say the appropriate number of '*bongs*' each time.

Step 2

1 If necessary, remind pupils of the mouse and the clock. Give each pupil worksheet 1. Pupils colour the clock and hands, (stick them onto card) and cut them out. Make centre holes using a hole punch or pencil. Attach hands using brass pins. Pupils colour in, cut out and stick the mouse to the end of a pencil.

2 Pupils work in pairs, using their clocks to ask *What time is it, please?* and adjusting their clocks each time, according to their partner's answers.

3 Use your blown-up clock and mouse to remind pupils of the words of the song. Say *Now let's sing the whole song*. Pupils sing along, moving the clock hands to the right time for each verse or 'bonging' the mouse on the clock face as appropriate.

Step 3

1 Put the hands of the blown-up clock to 6 o'clock. Say *What time is it?* Mime 'waking up' and 'getting out of bed'. Say *Listen. I get up at 6 o'clock*. Repeat with different times for *have breakfast / go to school / have lunch / go home / play on the computer / have dinner / go to bed?* Drill.

2 Give each pupil worksheet 2 and stick the A3 copy on the board. Using the picture at the top, drill *What time do you get up?* Get a pupil to ask you the question. Answer *I get up at 6 o'clock*. Draw the clock hands at 6 o'clock in the 'Me' column. Continue down the worksheet until all the questions and answers have been established and drilled and the 'Me' column completed.

3 Say *Now fill in the 'Me' column for you*. Check pupils are filling in information about themselves.

4 Write a pupil's name at the top of the second column. Ask him/her *What time do you get up? What time do you have breakfast?* and fill in the clocks appropriately.

5 Pupils work in groups of four or in a whole class mingle. Say *Ask three people about their day*. Pupils ask each other questions to complete their sheet.

6 Individual pupils tell the class what they discovered about their classmates e.g. *Richard gets up at 8 o'clock. He has lunch at 12 o'clock.*

Colour and make the clock and the mouse. Sing the song.

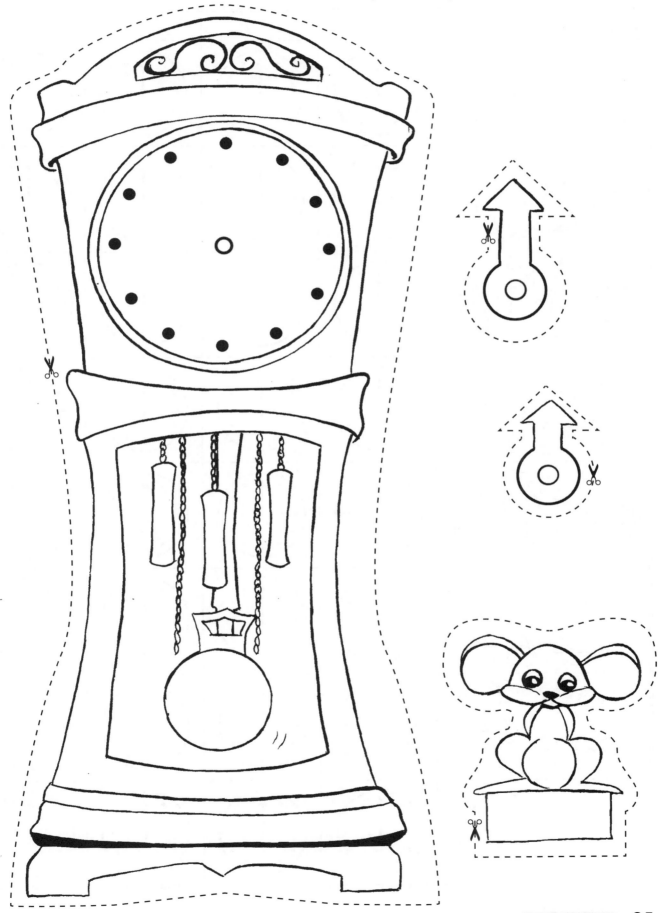

Complete the clocks for yourself. Then ask your friends *What time do you … ?*

What time do you … ?	Me			

Dingle dangle scarecrow

1.4

LANGUAGE FOCUS
things on a farm
parts of the body

LEVEL 1

AGE RANGE 6–8

TIME
Step 1: 20 minutes
Step 2: 35 minutes
Step 3: 15 minutes

MATERIALS
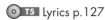 Lyrics p.127

Step 1
1 x A3 picture of a farm, flashcards of blown-up pictures from worksheet 1, a completed scarecrow made from worksheet 2, worksheet 1 for each pupil, scissors

Step 2
A completed scarecrow, worksheet 2 for each pupil, flashcards from worksheet 1, scissors, colouring pencils, a pencil or hole punch for making holes, brass pins for each pupil, sticky tape, pencils

Step 3
Colouring pencils, paper for pupils' pictures

FOLLOW-UP ACTIVITIES
Class sing the song about other parts of the body (p.14)

Class categorise pictures of the town and country and compare them: *fields/ buildings; clean/dirty; quiet/ noisy*, etc.

Step 1 Learning farm vocabulary, listening to and acting out the song
Step 2 Making a scarecrow, learning the song and singing it
Step 3 Countryside picture dictation

Step 1

1 Stick the picture of a farm to the board. Say *What is it?* (a farm). Say *What can you see on a farm?* Accept any animal words, as well as *tractor, farmer, field, tree, river,* etc.

2 Show pupils the 'sun' card from worksheet 1. Say *What is it?* (It's the sun.) Drill if necessary. Do the same with the 'moon', 'cows', 'hat', 'hens' and 'cloud' cards.

3 Say *Now it's night-time,* and hide the sun slowly behind the farm picture. Say *What's the sun doing?* Close your eyes and mime. (It's sleeping.) Say *Where do we sleep?* (in bed). Say *Yes. The sun's in bed.* Elicit the fact that the cows and hens are also sleeping.

4 Lift the moon and cloud cards up above the farm picture and say *Where's the moon?* (behind a cloud).

5 Finally reveal the 'scarecrow' card and say *This is a scarecrow! He stands in the fields to scare away the birds.* Jiggle the big completed scarecrow around. Say *What's this scarecrow doing? Is he sleeping?* (No.) *What's he wearing on his head?* (A hat! A flippy-floppy hat!) *Is he eating?* (No.) *Is he dancing?* (Yes – he's shaking his arms and legs.)

6 Give each pupil worksheet 1 and some scissors. Say *Cut out the cards carefully.*

7 Now say *Let's listen to the song. When you hear the words, hold your cards up. Shake the scarecrow's arms and legs.* Demonstrate with verse 1 of the song and the 'cows', 'sun', 'hat' and 'scarecrow' cards. Play the whole song for pupils to hold up the correct cards.

Step 2

1 Show pupils the completed scarecrow. Say *Let's make a Dingle dangle scarecrow!*

2 Give each pupil worksheet 2. Pupils colour in the scarecrow's head and body, arms, legs and hat, and cut them out.

3 Using a hole punch or pencil make holes in the scarecrow. Help pupils attach the arms, legs and hat with brass pins.

4 Attach pencils to the back of the scarecrows with sticky tape.

5 Teach pupils the chorus of the song *I'm a dingle, dangle scarecrow,* etc. Get them to move the scarecrow as though he is singing the song.

6 Use the flashcards from worksheet 1 to remind pupils of the words in the two verses. Stick them on the board. Play the song once to help pupils learn the words. Finally, get the class to stand up and sing the whole song, while acting it out. (If you feel the verses are too much to learn, pupils could simply do the actions and just sing the chorus.)

Step 3

1 Do a countryside picture dictation (p.15). Give each pupil a piece of paper and dictate instructions e.g. *Draw a farmhouse with four windows. Draw some trees. Draw some hens sleeping. Draw a big moon in the sky,* etc.

2 Remind pupils of other 'farm' words for them to add to their pictures.

3 Pupils compare their pictures, colour them and stick them on the wall. Ask questions about them e.g. *How many hens are there? What is the cow doing?*

Cut out the cards. Listen to the song and hold up the cards.

 Primary Music Box © Cambridge University Press 2010

Cut out and make the scarecrow. Sing the song.

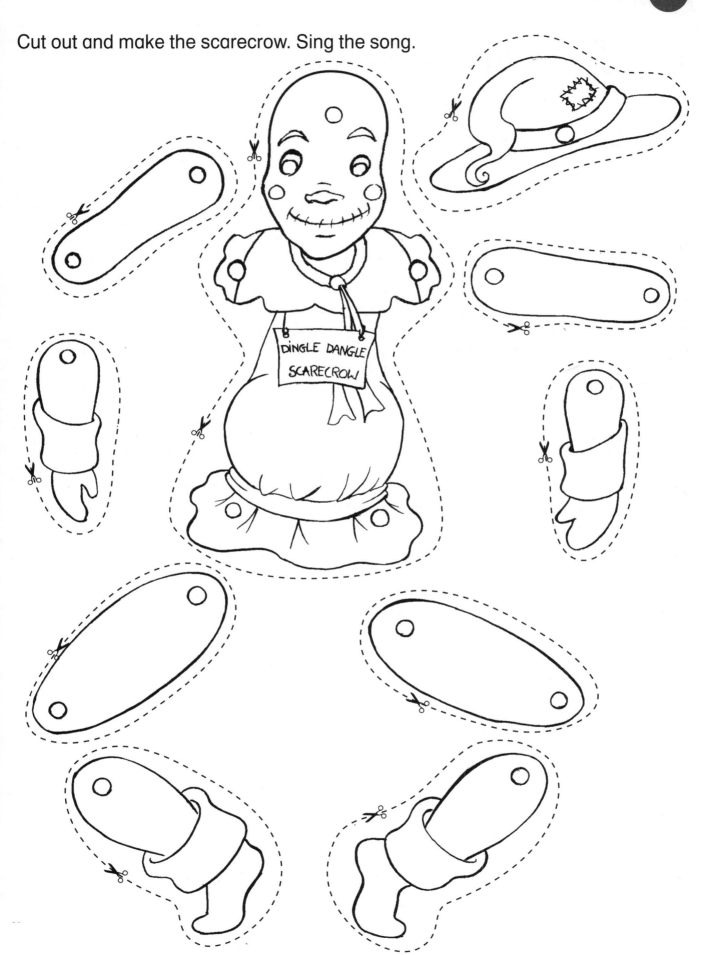

DINGLE DANGLE
SCARECROW

The music man

LANGUAGE FOCUS
musical instruments
Can you/he/she ... ?,
I can ...

LEVEL 1

AGE RANGE 6–8

TIME
Step 1: 10–15 minutes
Step 2: 20 minutes
Step 3: 25 minutes

MATERIALS
🎵 **T6** Lyrics p.128

Step 1
Flashcards of blown-up
pictures of completed
instruments from worksheet 1

Step 2
Worksheet 1 for each pupil
plus 1 x A3 copy completed,
(colouring pencils)

Step 3
Worksheet 2 for each
pupil plus 1 x A3 copy,
magazine pictures of musical
instruments, glue, scissors

**FOLLOW-UP
ACTIVITIES**
Pupils mime different
instruments and the class
guess what they are

Class add new instruments to
the song and create mimes to
go with them (p.14)

Step 1	Learning the names of musical instruments and related actions, listening to the song
Step 2	'Joining the dots' to make instruments, learning the song and singing it with actions
Step 3	Learning about the way that different instrument 'families' are played

Step 1

1 Stick flashcards of the *piano, violin, big bass drum, saxophone* and *triangle* from worksheet 1 onto your jacket or shirt. Say *I am the music woman/man!* Drill with the whole class *What can you play?* Get a pupil to point to one of the pictures e.g. the violin, and say *What can you play?* Mime playing the violin and say *I can play the violin.* Pupils mime and repeat. Repeat with the other instruments.

2 Mime an instrument and say *What can I play?* Pupils guess.

3 Say *Now, who can mime?* Pupils mime individually. Say *What can he/she play?* The other pupils put their hands up to guess. Correct pronunciation.

4 Say *Now listen to this song. When you hear an instrument, do a mime!* After the song, get pupils to come to the board and stick the instruments in the order of the song.
Key piano, violin, bass drum, saxophone, triangle

Step 2

1 Give each pupil worksheet 1. Say *Join the dots to find the instruments.* Monitor.

2 Use the A3 copy of worksheet 1 to check, by eliciting the names. Get pupils to number the order of the instruments in the song, playing it if necessary. Check.
Key 1 piano, 2 violin, 3 bass drum, 4 saxophone, 5 triangle

3 Say *How does the music man say the instruments in the song?* Play the recording again and teach/elicit *the pia – pia – piano, piano, piano; the vio – vio – violin, violin, violin; boom, boom, the big bass drum, the big bass drum, the big bass drum; the saxo – saxo – saxophone, saxophone, saxophone, ting, ting, ting, the triangle,* doing the actions at the same time.

4 Establish the format of the song with the music man introducing himself and his instruments *I am the music man, I come from down your way / I can play the ...* and someone asking the question *What can you play?*

5 Say *Now let's sing the song and do the actions!* Play the recording, with you asking *What can you play?* each time. In confident classes, small groups of pupils can take an instrument each.

6 (If time, pupils can colour the instruments on worksheet 1.)

Step 3

1 Give each pupil a copy of worksheet 2. Stick the A3 copy of worksheet 2 on the board. Say *Look at the pictures. Who's playing the piano?* Establish which silhouette is playing the piano. Repeat for the violin, saxophone and bass drum. For each one, establish how the instrument is played.

2 Say *Can you find another instrument that you play like the piano?* (keyboard). Get pupils to draw lines until all the instruments in the centre of the worksheet have been linked with their 'player'. Monitor.
Key piano – c; drum – b, f, i; saxophone – d, e; violin – a, g, h. (The violin and double bass have strings and can be plucked or played with a bow. The harp and guitar are plucked with the fingers only.)

3 Give pupils appropriate magazine pictures to cut out and stick in the columns next to the silhouettes or get them to draw in instruments of their own.

4 Ask pupils *Can you play the piano / saxophone,* etc. and teach *Yes I can / No I can't.*

Join the dots. What are the instruments? Write their number in the song.

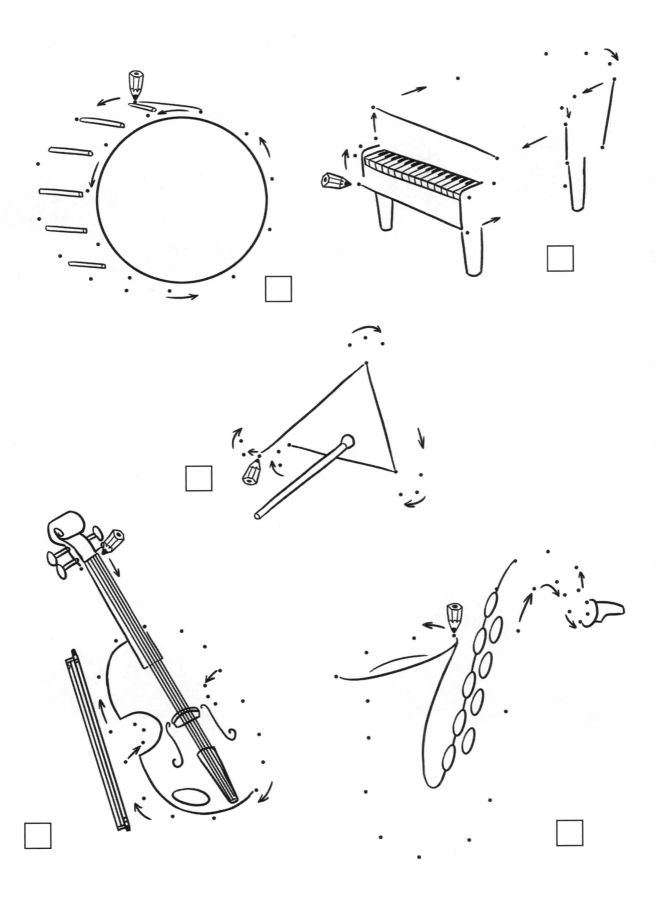

Draw lines from the instruments to the way we play them. Then add more pictures in the empty boxes.

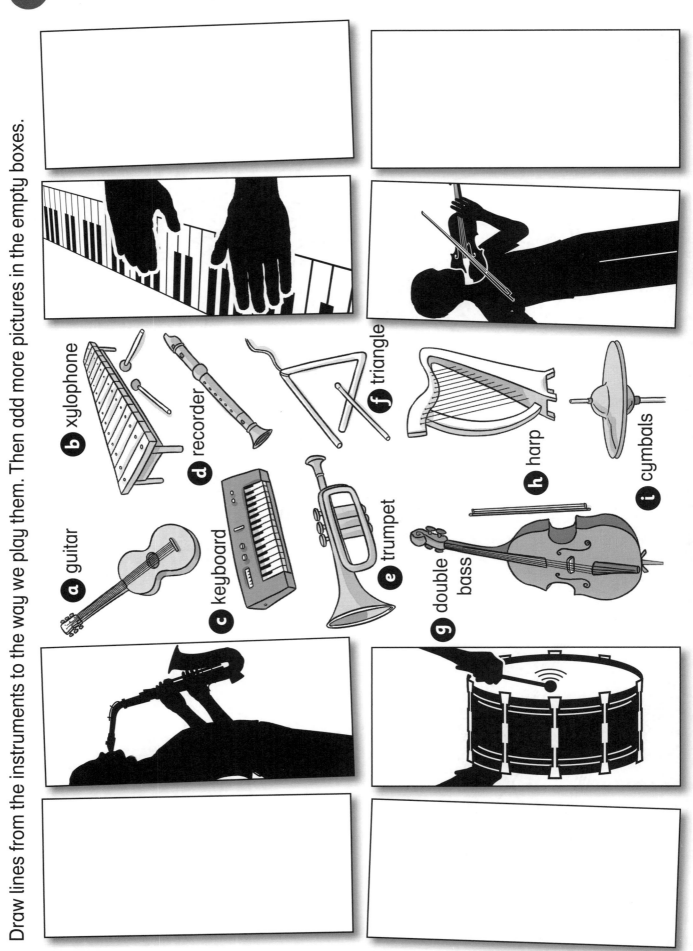

a guitar

b xylophone

c keyboard

d recorder

e trumpet

f triangle

g double bass

h harp

i cymbals

We wish you a Merry Christmas

LANGUAGE FOCUS
features and customs of a
traditional Christmas

LEVEL 1

AGE RANGE 6–8

TIME
Step 1: 15 minutes
Step 2: 25 minutes
Step 3: 30 minutes

MATERIALS
 Lyrics p.128

Step 2
Worksheet 1 for each pair of
pupils, cut in half

Step 3
Worksheet 2 for each pupil,
scissors, card, glue, string or
thread, colouring pencils

**FOLLOW-UP
ACTIVITIES**

Do a picture dictation based
on a Christmas scene (p.15)

Pupils draw a picture of food
they enjoy eating on a special
day

Step 1 Reviewing/Learning Christmas lexis and learning and singing the song

Step 2 'Spot the difference' activity practising 'Christmas' lexis, singing the song

Step 3 Making Christmas decorations

Step 1

1 Say *What days are special?* Elicit any public holidays, birthdays and religious days.

2 Say *What do we do on these days?* Elicit/Teach *have parties, give presents, visit family, eat special food, sing, dance,* etc.

3 Write *25th December* on the board. Say *What special day is this?* (*Christmas Day*). Repeat for *1st January* (*New Year's Day*). Say that a long time ago in Britain at Christmas, people walked to their friends' houses, singing. It was cold and people gave them nice things to eat and drink.

4 Say *Let's listen to a song that people sing at Christmas. What do they say to their friends?* Pupils listen to the first verse. Elicit *We wish you a Merry Christmas and a Happy New Year.* (*good tidings = good news; kin = family*). Teach and practise the words and get pupils to hold their arms wide in friendship.

5 Pupils listen to verse 2 for what the singers want (*some figgy (fruit) pudding and a cup of good cheer* (*happiness*). Get them to hold their hands out for food. Play verse 3. Say *What are the people saying?* (*We won't go until we get some, so bring some out here*). Get them to fold their arms and stamp their feet.

6 Play the whole song for pupils to sing the first and last verse and do actions to all the verses.

Step 2

1 If necessary, remind pupils of the song *We wish you a Merry Christmas.*

2 Put pupils into pairs. Give each pair one copy of worksheet 1, Picture A. Elicit/Teach *present, Christmas tree, snowman, Christmas pudding, holly, cracker, bell, star, snowing, Father Christmas, curtain, window, garden, lorry, rocket.* Practise/Check the lexis and concepts with questions like *Where are the presents?* (*under the Christmas tree*), *Who brings the presents?* (*Father Christmas*), *What's on the Christmas tree?* (*a star, bells*).

3 Give each pair of pupils one copy of worksheet 1, Picture B. Say *Look. In picture A there are crackers on the table but in picture B there are no crackers on the table. The pictures are different. Can you find nine more different things?* In pairs, pupils compare pictures. Elicit the other nine differences.
Key 1A/B There are crackers / no crackers on the table; 2A/B The snowman's got / hasn't got a hat on; 3A/B The Christmas pudding has / hasn't got holly on it; 4A/B Father Christmas is / isn't eating Christmas pudding; 5A/B Two children are / One boy is opening presents; 6A/B The boy's got a lorry and a rocket / a lorry; 7A/B There's a star / no star on the Christmas tree; 8A/B There are 9 / 12 bells on the tree; 9A/B The curtains are long / short; 10A/B It's snowing / not snowing in the garden

4 (If time, play and sing the song again.)

Step 3

1 Say *Let's make some Christmas decorations.*

2 Give each pupil worksheet 2. Elicit the words *present, Christmas pudding, snowman, bell, cracker, star.* Help the class to stick the worksheet on card and colour, cut out and put string or thread through the decorations.

3 Hang the decorations around the room or let pupils take them home.

Find the ten differences between Picture A and Picture B.

Picture A

✂ -

Picture B

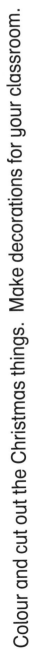

Colour and cut out the Christmas things. Make decorations for your classroom.

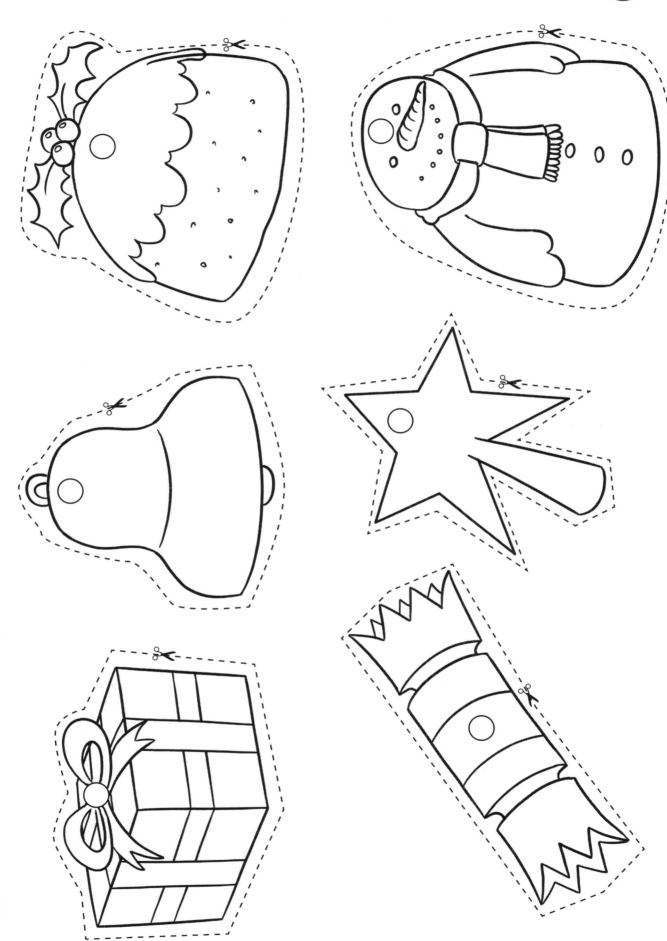

1.7

Bingo

LANGUAGE FOCUS
the alphabet, spelling

LEVEL 1

AGE RANGE 7–8

TIME
Step 1: 20 minutes
Step 2: 30 minutes
Step 3: 25 minutes

MATERIALS
T8 Lyrics p.129

Step 1
Flashcards of blown-up pictures of the farmer and his dog from worksheet 2

Step 2
Worksheet 1 copied enough times for each pair of pupils to have one 'Bingo card'

Step 3
Worksheet 2 for each pupil to cut up, scissors, (worksheet 2 for each pupil to keep as a record), (1 x A3 copy of worksheet 2 for the classroom wall)

FOLLOW-UP ACTIVITIES
Class make up new five-letter names for the dog and sing the song using them (p.14)

Class make a word snake around the room with their cut-out letters (p.15)

Step 1 Reviewing/Learning the pronunciation and written form of the alphabet, listening to verse 1 of the song
Step 2 Playing spelling Bingo, learning the song and singing it
Step 3 Playing spelling games

Step 1

1 Say *Who knows the alphabet?* Pupils come to the board in teams. Give each team a board pen. Each team member writes one letter of the alphabet, then the pen passes round the team until it is complete. Compare and correct. Establish a clear version for pupils to copy into their books. Drill.

2 Hold up the flashcards. Say *Let's listen to a song about this farmer and his dog.* Say *What's the dog's name?* Accept any answers. Play verse 1 of the song and elicit *Bingo.*

3 Say *How do you spell Bingo?* Pupils spell aloud. Say *Who can spell their name?* Pupils come to the board to write their names and spell them aloud.

4 (If time, play Hangman (p.15))

Step 2

1 Say *What's the farmer's dog's name?* (*Bingo*). Say *Now let's play a game called Bingo.*

2 Copy a 'bingo card' onto the board. Without saying the word itself, spell one of the words and cross it off to demonstrate. Continue with the other words. Say *When all the words have a cross, say Bingo!*

3 Put pupils into pairs. Give each pair one 'bingo card' from worksheet 1. Using this word list, spell words at random, crossing them off as you do so. **Do not** say the word itself, just the letters. When a pair say *Bingo!*, they are the winners.
alphabet, apple, boy, bus, car, cat, dog, doll, egg, elephant, fish, giraffe, girl, hen, house, insect, jacket, kite, leg, monkey, mouse, nose, number, orange, pencil, potato, queen, radio, robot, sun, tennis, train, umbrella, violin, watch, window, xylophone, yellow, yoyo, zebra, zoo

4 Ask the winners to say the words on their card to check. Check meanings, if appropriate.

5 Say *Now let's sing the song together.* Replace B,I,N,G and O with claps as shown in the song lyrics.

Step 3

1 Give each pupil worksheet 2. Say *What word begins with 'a'?* (*apple*) *What word begins with 'n'?* (*nose*). Do the same for other letters at random.

2 Say *Cut up all the letters and mix them up.* Pupils do this. Say *Now put the letters in order as fast as you can. a, b, c … .* Pupils race to put the letters in alphabetical order.

3 Say *Now let's spell some words with our letters.* Say *Spell 'zebra'.* Pairs of pupils spell it with their letters. Dictate other words from worksheet 2. Make the exercise more difficult by choosing words from any of the bingo cards from worksheet 1. Get pupils to write them on the board to check.

4 In pairs pupils say words for each other to spell using their two sets of letters.

5 Give each pupil a new whole copy of worksheet 2 to keep (and/or stick the A3 version on the classroom wall).

Bingo 1

Play Bingo.

1

fish	girl	kite	cat	kite	zebra
train	number	watch	radio	orange	robot
leg	nose	giraffe	car	leg	watch

3 / **4**

bus	nose	dog	robot	doll	alphabet
hen	kite	window	nose	zebra	pencil
watch	umbrella	doll	apple	queen	zoo

5 / **6**

pencil	girl	watch	doll	girl	egg
tennis	zebra	train	giraffe	elephant	robot
sun	doll	potato	insect	kite	pencil

7 / **8**

train	window	robot	watch	jacket	girl
egg	tennis	apple	house	hen	bus
watch	xylophone	yoyo	yoyo	doll	yellow

9 / **10**

boy	mouse	nose	number	violin	egg
pencil	bus	robot	hen	bus	cat
leg	monkey	yoyo	robot	house	nose

Cut out the letters of the alphabet and make words.

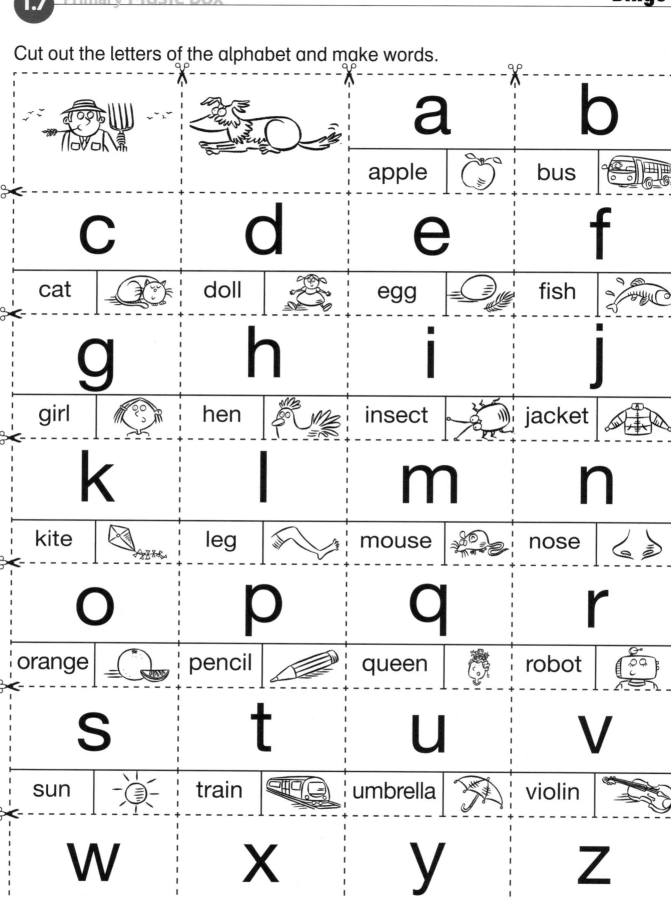

Old Macdonald had a farm

LANGUAGE FOCUS
farm animals
animal sounds
animal products

LEVEL 1

AGE RANGE 7–8

TIME
Step 1: 20 minutes
Step 2: 20 minutes
Step 3: 25 minutes

MATERIALS

 Lyrics p.129

Step 1
1 x A3 copy of Old
Macdonald and the dog from
the bottom of worksheet 1,
flashcards of blown-up copies
of all the animals in
worksheet 1, recording on
CD (after song) of animal
noises

Step 2
Worksheet 1 for each pupil

Step 3
Products / pictures of
products from farm animals
e.g. woollen scarf, leather
belt, watchstrap, wallet,
purse, bag, or food products
(avoid those in worksheet
2), worksheet 2 for each
pupil plus 1 x A3 copy,
(supermarket magazines,
wall-chart size card, scissors,
glue)

**FOLLOW-UP
ACTIVITIES**

Class play Guess the animal
with animals from worksheet 1
(p.16)

Class make a poster ranking
farm animals from smallest to
largest, adding new animals
if appropriate (p.16)

Step 1 Reviewing/Learning the names of animals and the sounds they make, listening to the song

Step 2 Matching pictures of animals and their sounds, spelling and writing animal names, learning the song and singing it with actions

Step 3 Making a chart showing what animals give us

Step 1

1 Hold up the A3 copy of Old Macdonald and the dog. Say *What's he?* (*a farmer*). Drill his name. Say *What animals live on Old Macdonald's farm?* Accept all suggestions. When pupils mention one of *cow, duck, sheep, pig, horse, cat,* stick the flashcard of that animal on the board. Elicit/Teach all the animals and drill.

2 Say *Listen to this song.* Play verse 1. Say *What animal has Old Macdonald got on his farm?* (*a cow*). Put the cow on the left of the board. Repeat for all verses. Get pupils to order the animal pictures on the board according to the order in the song.
Key cow, duck, sheep, pig, (cow)

3 Using the animal noise after the song recording, say *What animal makes this noise?* (*moo moo – a cow*). Do the same with the other animals. **Key** cow – *moo, moo,* sheep – *baa,* cat – *miaow,* duck – *quack, quack;* horse – *neigh;* pig – *oink, oink*
Check by saying an animal name and getting the pupils to make the noise or vice versa.

4 Play the song again, stopping before each animal noise for pupils to make the noise.

Step 2

1 Give each pupil worksheet 1. Say *The cow goes moo moo. Can you see the line? Now you draw lines for the animals.* Pupils do this and compare. Check.
Key see 3 in Step 1

2 Write the name of an animal on the board with the letters jumbled e.g. *a t c.* Say *What's this animal?* (*cat*). Pupils label the 'cat' picture on worksheet 1. Write the other jumbled names on the board. Put pupils into pairs to order letters and find the words. Establish correct spellings on the board. Pupils copy onto worksheet 1.

3 Say *Let's sing Old Macdonald had a farm!* Drill verse 1 and perform the following actions: (*with a moo moo here / here a moo* – point to somewhere near you; *and a moo moo there* – point to far away; *everywhere a moo moo* – open your arms to indicate *everywhere.*) Play the whole song, with pupils following the order of the first four animals on the worksheet, making the noises and doing the actions. (If time, sing two more verses with *horse* and *cat.*)

Step 3

1 Hold up your objects or pictures of animal products. For each one say *What animal does this come from?* and elicit the names of the animals.

2 Give each pupil worksheet 2. Say *What comes from a sheep?* Using the A3 copy of worksheet 2, point out the woolly hats next to the sheep. Repeat with *cow* and show the carton of milk. Show pupils the objects and words round worksheet 2. Say *Draw these things next to the animals they come from.* Monitor and check.
Key sheep – hats, meat, cheese, jumpers, rugs; cow – milk, shoes, meat, cheese, butter; hen – eggs, feathers, meat

3 Say *Do you have anything that comes from an animal?* Pupils show and name any woollen or leather items. Say *Can you think of any other things?* Draw them on the board with their names for pupils to add to their diagrams.

(If time, use magazine pictures of animal products to make a large class poster.)

What do the animals say? Draw lines. Then write the animals' names.

cow

Old Macdonald had a farm 2

What do animals give us? Draw the things next to the correct animal.

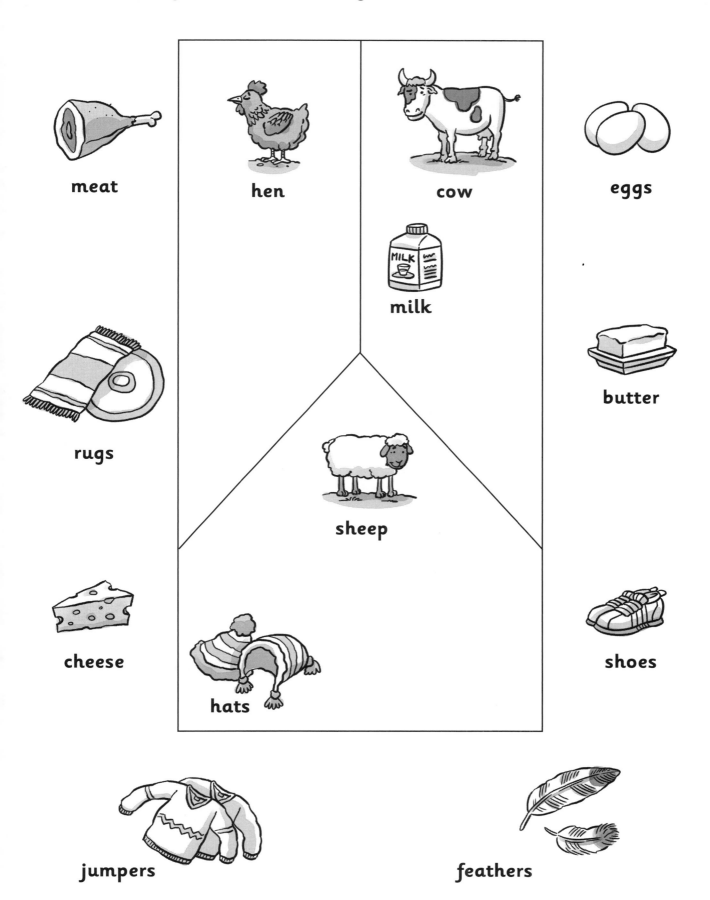

meat

hen

cow

eggs

milk

rugs

butter

sheep

cheese

hats

shoes

jumpers

feathers

If you're happy and you know it

LANGUAGE FOCUS
parts of the body and actions
If you're ... , + imperative

LEVEL 1

AGE RANGE 7-8

TIME
Step 1: 20 minutes
Step 2: 35 minutes
Step 3: 20 minutes

MATERIALS
🔘 **110** Lyrics p.130

Step 2
Worksheet 1 for each pupil,
(card, glue), scissors

Step 3
Worksheet 2 for each pupil
plus 1 x A3 copy

FOLLOW-UP ACTIVITIES
Pupils label the parts of the body of the figures from worksheet 1

Pupils make illustrated posters using information from the survey (p.16)

Step 1	Reviewing/Learning names for parts of the body and action verbs, listening to the song and doing actions
Step 2	Singing the song with actions, playing a 'parts of the body' card game
Step 3	Class survey on 'What makes you happy?'

Step 1

1 Draw a man on the board. Say *Where's his head?* Pupils point. Label his head. Repeat for *feet, hands, legs, arms, nose, eyes, ears, body, neck, hair* and *mouth*. Drill. Check by touching parts of your body and eliciting the words.

2 Say *Listen to this song.* Play verse 1. Say *What did it say?* Elicit *If you're happy and you know it, clap your hands.* Establish meaning. Say *Clap your hands.* Pupils do the action.

3 For each verse, establish which body part is mentioned and what to do (*stamp your feet (stamp, stamp), nod your head (nod, nod), touch your nose (beep, beep), say I am! (I am!).* Mix up the instructions to check understanding.

4 Play the whole song. Pupils do the actions.

Step 2

1 If necessary, say *Can you remember the happy song?* Elicit the parts of the body in order on the board (*hands, feet, head, nose*). Drill them and the actions that go with them. Pupils sing and act out the song.

2 Give each pupil worksheet 1. Say *Look at these happy people.* Point to the *fireman* and say *What's he?* Repeat with *nurse* and *clown*.

3 Say *Cut up the people into six cards.* (If time, get pupils to stick the pictures onto card first.)

4 Use four pupils to demonstrate the card game. Mix their 72 cards. Deal twelve to each pupil. Place the remainder in a pile face down on the table.

5 Each pupil makes as much as possible of the fireman, the clown and the nurse from the cards they have. The aim is to make two whole characters.

6 Player 1 takes a card from the pile and says what it is e.g. *This is the fireman's feet.* If they can use the card, they keep it and put another one of their cards face down at the bottom of the pile on the table. If not, they replace it under the pile.

7 Player 2 takes a card, identifies it e.g. *This is the nurse's arms* and either uses or discards the card, and so on. The winner is the first player to construct two complete characters.

Step 3

1 Say *What makes you happy?* Draw a cat on the board. Smile and say *Cats make me happy!* Draw rain and an umbrella and frown and say *Rain doesn't make me happy.*

2 Give each pupil worksheet 2. Stick the A3 copy of worksheet 2 on the board. Point to the first question and drill *What food makes you happy?* Point to the ice cream picture and say *Ice cream makes me happy.* Drill the other questions and reply for yourself, drawing any appropriate item in each column.

3 Get pupils to write in a final question e.g. *What music/place/day/ ... ?*

4 Say *Draw pictures of what makes you happy in the 'Me' column.* Monitor.

5 Say *Now ask three people what makes them happy.* Pupils ask three of their classmates the questions, write their names and draw pictures on the worksheet.

6 Pupils report back to the class about the people they interviewed. *Water makes Monica happy. / Watching television makes Monica happy. / Monica's brother makes her happy,* etc.

Cut up the people to make a card game.

Ask your friends *What makes you happy?*

	Me	Name	Name	Name
What food makes you happy?				
What drink makes you happy?				
What colour makes you happy?				
What animal makes you happy?				
What toy makes you happy?				
What hobby makes you happy?				
Who makes you happy?				
What _____ makes you happy?				

There was an old lady

LANGUAGE FOCUS
animals and what they eat

LEVEL 1

AGE RANGE 7–8

TIME
Step 1: 20 minutes
Step 2: 30 minutes
Step 3: 25 minutes

MATERIALS
Lyrics p.130

Step 1
Blown-up and cut-out animals and a completed 'old lady envelope' from worksheet 2, worksheet 1 for each pupil plus 1 x A3 copy

Step 2
Blown-up characters from worksheet 2, worksheet 2 for each pupil, scissors, glue, large separate pieces of card with the phrases: *I don't know why / That tickled and tickled and tickled inside her / How absurd! / Fancy that! / What a hog! / I don't know how! / She's dead, of course!*

Step 3
Poster card, blown-up characters from worksheet 2, pupils' cut-out characters from worksheet 2, glue, pens, colouring pencils

FOLLOW-UP ACTIVITIES

Do an animal picture dictation e.g. *Draw a big red spider. Give it green eyes,* etc. (p.15)

Class design a much healthier diet for the old lady for breakfast, lunch and dinner

Step 1 Reviewing/Learning the names of animals, following the story in the song
Step 2 Making the characters in the song, learning the song and singing it
Step 3 Making 'What do animals eat?' posters

Step 1

1 Stick the completed 'old lady envelope' on the board. Say *Who's this?* (an old lady).

2 Stick the A3 copy of the worksheet 1 'maze' on the board. Give each pupil a copy. Say *Where's the old lady?* Draw a circle round her.

3 Say *What animals can you see?* Teach and drill the animal words on worksheet 1.

4 Demonstrate *swallow*. Say *What did the old lady swallow?* Play verse 1 of the song. Elicit *a fly*. On the maze, circle the fly and draw a line between it and the old lady.

5 Say *What can eat the fly? What can she swallow now?* Get pupils to guess but don't say if they are correct. Play verse 2 to check (*a spider*). Pupils guess what comes next in each verse, then listen to the song and circle and join the animals to complete the chain.

6 Say *What did the old lady swallow?* Get pupils to come and stick the blown-up animals on the board in order.
   Key fly, spider, bird, cat, dog, cow, horse

7 Play the song again for pupils to check and follow their 'mazes'.

Step 2

1 If necessary, elicit the animals that the old lady swallowed.

2 Say *Let's make the old lady and the animals.* Give each pupil worksheet 2. Pupils cut the characters out. Demonstrate how to make the old lady envelope.

3 Say *What did the old lady swallow first?* (a fly). Say *Listen to the song. What does it say about the fly?* Play the first verse. Elicit *I don't know why* and do a suitable action. Stick the old lady and the fly on the board with the phrase *I don't know why* under the fly. Teach *Perhaps she'll die.*

4 Continue building up the order of the characters and the phrases with suitable actions to the end of the song.
   Key spider (*That tickled and tickled and tickled inside her*); bird (*How absurd!*); cat (*Fancy that!*); dog (*What a hog!*); cow (*I don't know how!*); horse (*She's dead of course!*).

5 Say *Let's sing the song and make the old lady swallow the animals.* Using the prompts on the board, pupils sing and put the animals into the old lady envelope.

Step 3

1 Write on the board *What do these animals eat in the song?*

2 Stick your cut-out animals and the old lady across the board in reverse order from the song (*old lady, horse, cow, dog, cat, bird, spider, fly*).

3 Point to the horse. Say *Do old ladies eat horses?* (*Sometimes. They eat meat.*) Write on the board *People eat meat.* Say *What else do they eat?* (*vegetables, bread,* etc.) Add pupils' suggestions to the *They eat meat* sentence. Point to the horse and the cow. Say *Do horses eat cows?* (*No!*) Elicit/Teach *grass.* Write on the board *Horses eat grass.*

4 Put pupils into pairs. They colour and stick their cut-out animals from Step 2 onto posters and write sentences (or draw pictures) about what they eat. Help with ideas. (*horses – hay, grass; dogs – meat, bones; cats – fish, small animals; birds – insects, worms, seeds; spiders – flies; flies – rubbish, old food, plants*). Pupils can add other animals e.g. rabbits, mice.

5 Pupils stick finished posters on the classroom walls.

What did the old lady swallow? Listen to the song and circle the animals. Draw lines to join them up.

duck	pig	cow	horse **Finish**
hen	dog	fish	giraffe
rabbit	sheep	cat	snake
frog	spider	bird	monkey
Start old lady	fly	tiger	elephant

There was an old lady 2

Cut out the animals and make the old lady. Listen and sing and give the old lady her food!

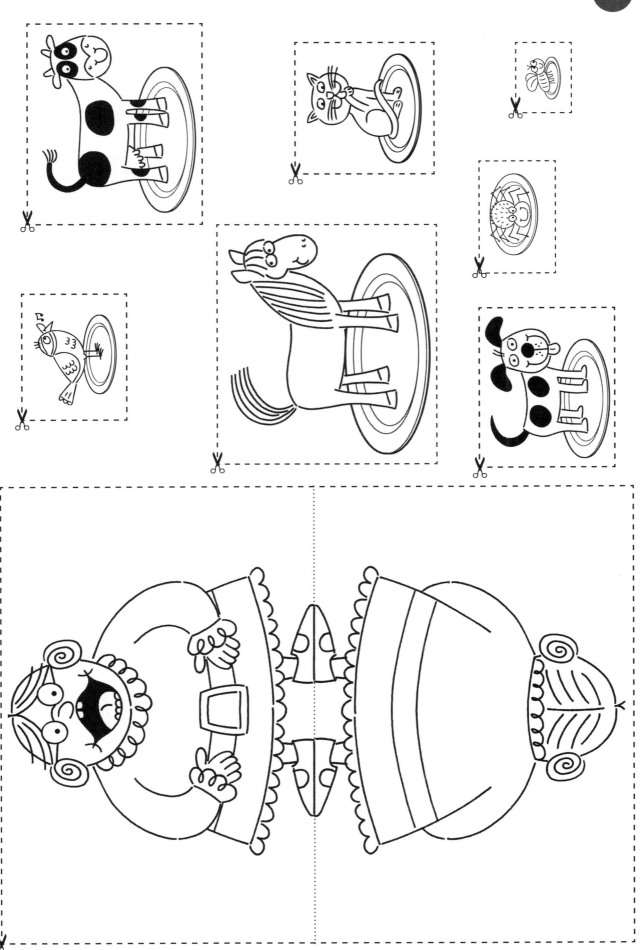

Here we go round the mulberry bush

LANGUAGE FOCUS
days of the week
daily activities
parts of the body
clothes

LEVEL 1

AGE RANGE 7–8

TIME
Step 1: 20 minutes
Step 2: 25 minutes
Step 3: 20 minutes

MATERIALS
 Lyrics p.131

Step 1
The 'picture' part of
worksheet 1 for each pupil
plus 1 x A3 copy

Step 2
Worksheet 1 for each pupil
plus 1 x A3 copy

Step 3
One 'person' and one word
box part of worksheet 2 for
each pupil, colouring pencils

**FOLLOW-UP
ACTIVITIES**
Class rewrite the song based
on the unused 'evening'
words in worksheet 1 (p.14)

Pupils write a description of
one of the funnily-dressed
people from worksheet 2

Step 1 Learning phrases for daily activities, listening to the song and doing the actions

Step 2 Learning/Reviewing days of the week, writing about daily routines, singing the song

Step 3 Learning/Reviewing clothes and parts of the body, creating funny people

Step 1

1 Write on the board. *It's 6 am.* Say *What time is it? Is it morning or evening?* (*early in the morning*).

2 Say *Listen. This song is about what people do early in the morning.* Play verse 1 only. Say *They're dancing round a little tree early in the morning.*

3 Give each pupil the 'picture' part of worksheet 1. Say *Look at the pictures. Put a circle round the things you do in the morning.* Pupils circle pictures for themselves.

4 Use the A3 picture to elicit and drill sentences for the pictures pupils have chosen. Combine drilling with suitable mime actions. Include the following from the song *Early in the morning we wash our face / comb our hair / brush our teeth / put on our clothes / go to school / tidy our rooms / stay in bed.* Check meaning by giving instructions for pupils to do the actions.

5 Say *Now listen to the song.* Play verse 2. Stop the recording. Say *What did they say?* Elicit *We wash our face.* Show pupils where to write a number 1 by the appropriate picture. Continue the song, filling in the numbers 2–7. Check answers. **Key** as in 4 above.

6 Play the song a final time for pupils to do the actions.

Step 2

1 Write the letters M, T, W, T, F, S and S vertically on the board. Say *What are these letters?* (*the first letters of the days of the week*). Elicit/Teach and drill *Monday, Tuesday,* etc.

2 Give each pupil the whole of worksheet 1. Say *In the mulberry bush song, what do we do on Monday early in the morning?* (*wash our face*). Use the A3 copy to show pupils how to complete the sentence for Monday morning, using the phrase from the box. Check and drill. (*On Monday morning we wash our face.*) Pupils circle the phrases in the word box that match the song.

3 Play the song several times while pupils write in the seven days of the week and the activities in the song. Monitor and check. Say *Now let's sing the song and do the actions.*

Step 3

1 Say *In the mulberry bush song, what do we do on Thursday morning?* (*put on our clothes*). Say *Let's play a dressing game.*

2 Put pupils into groups of four. Give each pupil one of the 'people' from worksheet 2.

3 Say *Don't show the others. Draw a face on your person and write a name in the box.* Then say *Put some things on your person's feet and colour them.* Pupils then fold the paper to cover what they've drawn and pass their 'person' to the next pupil, who draws and colours clothes on the person's legs and folds the paper again.

4 The 'person' goes to two more pupils in the group who each draw and colour clothes on the body, arms and hands / on the head. When all four stages are complete, each pupil receives their 'person' back and opens it out.

5 Give each pupil the 'words' part of worksheet 2. Drill and check meaning and pronunciation. In pairs, pupils describe their person to each other. *Maria's wearing blue and green socks, black shorts, a pink T-shirt and a hat with a frog on.* Monitor.

6 You could use the 2nd 'person' on the worksheet to repeat the activity, or for a picture dictation.

1 Circle the things you do in the mornings. Then listen and write numbers 1–7.

2 Complete the sentences about the week.

On Monday morning	we ....
On Tuesday	we ....
On Wed..	we ....
On T..	we ....
On	we ....
On	we ....
On	we ....

> wash our face / do our homework / listen to music / go to school / phone our friends / brush our teeth / eat dinner / stay in bed / comb our hair / read a book / put on our clothes / play games / watch TV / tidy our rooms

1 Play the dressing game.

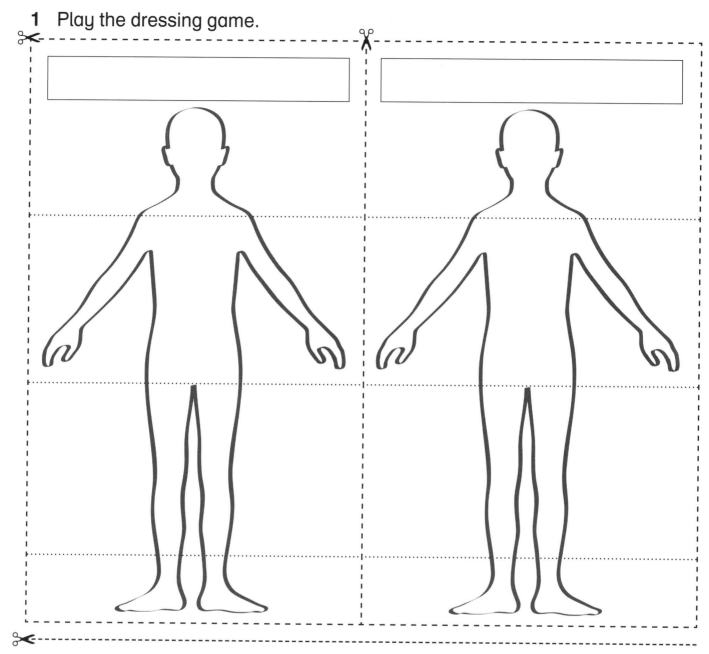

2 Use these words to talk about your person.

jacket

top

bag

shirt

trousers

glasses

skirt

hat

socks

watch

T-shirt

shorts

shoes

There was a princess long ago

LANGUAGE FOCUS
fairy tales

LEVEL 1

AGE RANGE 7–8

TIME
Step 1: 25 minutes
Step 2: 30 minutes
Step 3: 25 minutes

MATERIALS
🎵 **113** Lyrics p.131

Step 1
Worksheet 1 for each pupil
plus 1 x A3 copy

Step 2
Worksheet 2 for each pupil,
scissors, glue

Step 3
OHT/copy of song words
for each pupil with words
gapped (see point **1**)

**FOLLOW-UP
ACTIVITIES**
Pupils play Snap in groups
of three or four, using cut-
up cards from worksheet 1.
When two cards share an
element (e.g. trees, crown,
princess, etc.) the first pupil
to say that word (and not
'Snap') wins all the cards.
(p.15)

Class act out a favourite fairy
tale or story from their own
country (p.15)

Step 1 Learning lexis from the story, ordering pictures, listening to the song
Step 2 Making crowns, learning the song and acting it out
Step 3 Class write their own version of the song

Step 1

1 Draw or show pictures of a simple tower. Say *What is it?* Elicit/Teach *tower* and label it. Add further pictures to elicit/teach *window, princess, crown, forest, handsome prince, horse, fairy, wand, sword.* Teach *waved, riding, wake up, chopped, kissed, slept.*

2 Give each pupil worksheet 1. Describe picture *a*. Pupils work in pairs to try to describe the remaining pictures to each other. Then use the A3 version of worksheet 1 to check. Say *Who's this? What's he/she doing? Where is he/she?*, etc.

3 Say *Let's listen to the story.* Play verse 1 of the song. Say *What words did you hear?* (*princess*). Say *Which picture is it?* (*a*). Show the number *1* next to picture *a* as an example.

4 Put pupils into pairs and say *Now listen to the song and write numbers next to the pictures.* Play the song twice before checking.
Key 1a, 2f, 3g, 4b, 5d, 6i, 7c, 8h, 9e

Step 2

1 If necessary, remind pupils of the song. Say *Let's make crowns for the prince and princess!* Give each pupil worksheet 2. Show them how to cut their crowns out and stick them together.

2 Divide the class into groups of seven or eight pupils. Three pupils are the *beautiful princess*, the *handsome prince* and the *naughty fairy*. The rest stand in a circle round them. Elicit/ Teach the words of the verses with suitable actions:
- *There was a princess long ago* – 'princess' stands in centre. Others walk round her holding hands.
- *And she lived in a big, high tower* – circle lift arms up to show walls of tower round princess
- *A naughty fairy waved her wand* – 'fairy' goes into centre and waves her wand over the princess
- *The princess slept for a hundred years* – 'princess' lies down and sleeps
- *A great big forest grew around* – circle closes in on princess, waving arms like branches
- *A handsome prince came riding by* – 'prince' rides around outside of circle
- *He took his sword and chopped it down* – 'prince' chops through trees and goes to princess, trees collapse to their knees
- *He kissed her hand to wake her up* – 'prince' kisses princess' hand, she gets up
- *So everybody's happy now* – all hold hands and dance round.

3 Pupils change roles and act out the song to the music.

Step 3

1 Give out copies or make an OHT of the words of the song with one word from each verse missing. These words are: *princess, tower, fairy, slept, forest, prince, sword, hand, happy.*

2 Dictate or write the missing words on the board. Say *Put the words in the song.* Pupils do this and check together. Then check in whole class.

3 Say *Now let's change the song!* Write the line *There was a princess long ago* on the board and cross out the word *princess*. Say *What shall we write?* Accept any funny suggestions such as *teacher/pupil/robot*, etc. Continue with verse 2.

4 Pupils write their new songs in small groups or as a whole class, then sing them.

Listen and number the pictures.

c

f

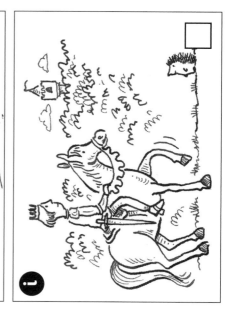

i

b

e

h

a

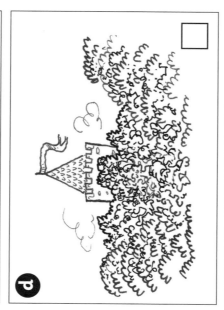

d

g

Make a crown for the prince or princess. Act out the song.

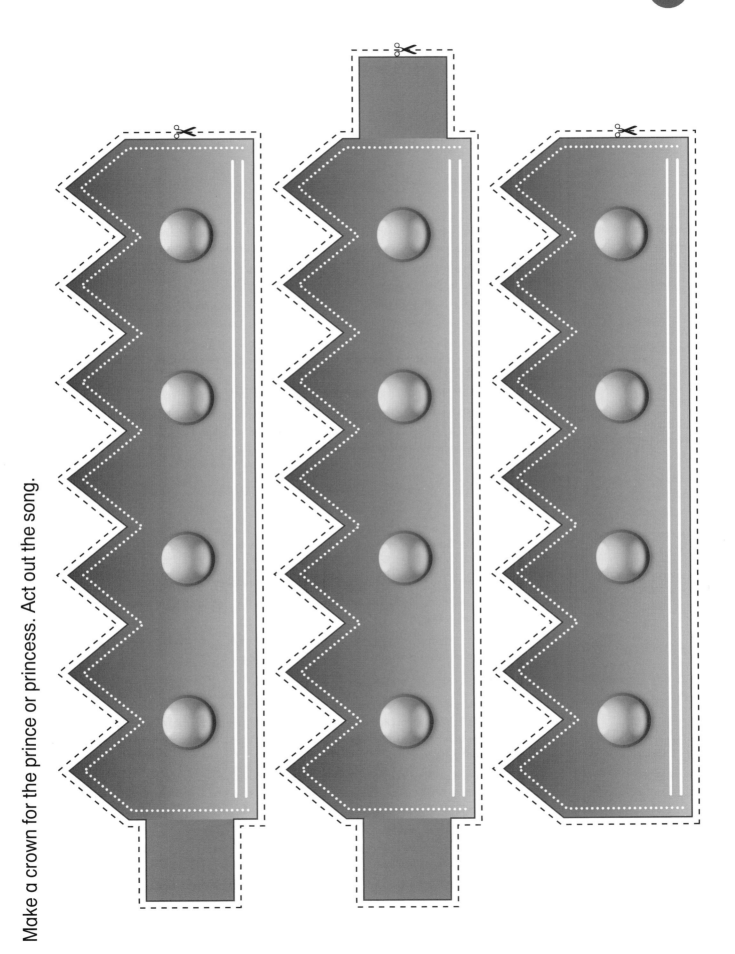

 2.1

The Hokey Cokey

LANGUAGE FOCUS
parts of the body and actions

LEVEL 2

AGE RANGE 7–10

TIME
Step 1: 20 minutes
Step 2: 25 minutes
Step 3: 30 minutes

MATERIALS

T14 Lyrics p.132

Step 1
Worksheet 1 for each pupil
plus 1 x A3 copy

Step 2
Worksheet 1 for each pupil
plus 1 x A3 copy

Step 3
Worksheet 2 for each pupil
plus 1 x A3 copy

FOLLOW-UP ACTIVITIES
Play Simon Says (p.15)

Explore the senses (p.16)

Step 1 Reviewing/Learning parts of the body, ticking correct pictures in verse 1 and chorus, learning actions
Step 2 Ordering the song verses, singing the song and doing the actions, drawing yourself in the picture
Step 3 Doing a 'body' crossword puzzle and picture dictation

Step 1

1 Say *We're going to learn a dance called the Hokey Cokey.* Elicit names for parts of the body and write them across the board. Include *arm, whole self, nose, ears, leg, knees.*

2 Elicit/Teach *left* and *right.* Get pupils to stand up. Say *Show me your right arm.* Demonstrate and check. Repeat with *left arm, right leg* and *left leg.*

3 Teach the words and actions (*wave, shake, bend, turn around, straight*). Call out instructions e.g. *Shake your left leg. Knees bend. Wave your hand. Put your right arm out straight,* etc.

4 Give each pupil worksheet 1 and stick the A3 copy on the board. Say *Listen and circle the pictures for the things you hear.* Play verse 1, pausing as necessary. Pupils circle the correct pictures. Check.
Key right arm, right arm, shake, turn around, knees, arms

5 Pupils stand in a circle. Play verse 1 and the chorus of the song. Pupils do the actions. For *You do the Hokey Cokey,* pupils roll arms over each other. For *Oh, oh, the Hokey Cokey,* pupils join hands and move in and out of the circle.

Step 2

1 If necessary, give each pupil worksheet 1 and elicit the name of the dance (*The Hokey Cokey*). Stick the A3 copy on the board.

2 Say *Look at what the children are singing.* Read the speech bubbles and point out the example. Say *Listen to the song and write numbers.* Play the recording. Check.
Key 1e, 2c, 3d, 4b, 5a

3 Pupils stand in a circle. Say *Let's sing and do the Hokey Cokey.*

4 While still in the circle, ask pupils for new ideas e.g. *left arm, right knee,* and sing them in the song.

5 Pupils sit down and write their favourite new instruction into the last speech bubble, then draw themselves doing that action in the empty box.

Step 3

1 If necessary, review body parts. Elicit also *toes, fingers, neck, shoulder, eyes, mouth, foot, hand* and *teeth.* Write them on the board and drill. Then play a Spot the Mistakes game e.g. Say *Bend your right knee* and do an opposite action. Pupils do the action for what you are saying, not what you are doing.

2 Give each pupil worksheet 2 and stick the A3 copy on the board. Say *This is a 'body' crossword.* Read the definition for 1 Across. Pupils find the matching picture (*mouth*). Point out the word *mouth* in the crossword. Pupils complete the crossword in pairs.

3 Elicit the correct answers and write the words on the board. Pupils check spelling.
Key Across: 1 mouth, 3 fingers, 6 hand, 8 teeth, 10 ear, 11 legs. Down: 2 toes, 3 foot, 4 nose, 5 shoulder, 7 neck, 9 eye

4 Do a picture dictation. Read out this text, using the crossword numbers or the words. *This is a funny monster. He's got a big head. He's got a long 7 down (neck). He's got small 9 down (eyes) and a big 4 down (nose). He's got a small body. He's got long 11 across (legs). He's got big 6 across (hands) and long 3 across (fingers). He's got small 3 down (feet).* Pupils listen and draw, then compare their pictures.

1 Listen and circle the words in the song.

You put your left leg / right arm in, your right arm / left foot out,

In, out, in, out, wave shake it all about.

You do the Hokey Cokey and you jump about / turn around ,

That's what it's all about!

Oh, oh, the Hokey Cokey!

Oh, oh, the Hokey Cokey!

Oh, oh, the Hokey Cokey!

Arms / Knees bent, arms / knees straight, ra, ra, ra!

2 Look at what the children are singing. Listen and number. Then write your own line for the song.

a You put your whole self in. ☐

b You put your one nose in. ☐

c You put your left leg in. ☐

d You put your two ears in. ☐

e You put your right arm in. 1

You put your .... in.

Read the clues and find the pictures. Then write the words in the crossword puzzle.

Across

1 You put food in this.

3 You've got five of these on your hand.

6 This is at the end of your arm.

8 You bite an apple with these.

10 You hear with this.

11 You run with these.

Down

2 You've got five of these on your foot.

3 This is at the end of your leg.

4 You smell flowers with this.

5 This is at the top of your arm.

7 This is between your head and your body.

9 You see with this.

1 Across

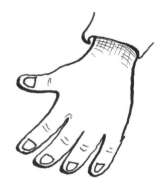

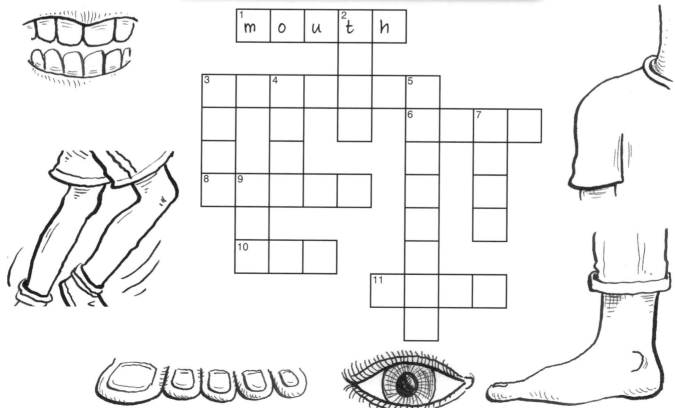

Kookaburra

2.2

LANGUAGE FOCUS
Australian animals and
geographical features
describing animals *It's got ... ,
It can ...*

LEVEL 2

AGE RANGE 8–10

TIME
Step 1: 25 minutes
Step 2: 15 minutes
Step 3: 20 minutes

MATERIALS
🔘**115** Lyrics p.132

Step 1
World map or globe, pictures
of kangaroo, emu, crocodile,
koala, worksheet 1 and a
piece of blank paper for
each pupil, some 'gum drop'
sweets

Step 2
Worksheet 1 for each pupil,
(colouring pencils, gum
drops)

Step 3
Worksheet 2 for each pupil
plus 1 x A3 copy

**FOLLOW-UP
ACTIVITIES**
Play Guess the animal (p.16)

Pupils create their own fact
card about an animal

Step 1 Reviewing/Learning about Australia and its animals, drawing a kookaburra, listening to the song and ordering pictures
Step 2 Gap-filling and singing the song
Step 3 Describing animals, filling in Australian animal fact cards

Step 1

1 Say *We're going to listen to a song about Australia.* Show Australia on your map or globe.

2 Ask questions about Australia. *Is Australia a small country? What Australian cities do you know?* Say *What is the Australian countryside called?* Teach *bush.*

3 Say *What animals live in the Australian bush?* Write suggestions on the board. Include *kangaroo, koala, emu,* and *crocodile* and show the pictures. Say *kookaburra,* but don't show a picture.

4 Say *Listen to a kookaburra.* Play the kookaburra's call on the recording. Say *Is he happy or sad?* (*happy*). *Why?* (*He's laughing!*)

5 Give each pupil some blank paper and say *Now draw the kookaburra.* Pupils draw their imaginary animal and compare.

6 Give each pupil worksheet 1. Pupils compare their drawings with the kookaburra.

7 Using the worksheet, say *Where does the kookaburra live?* (*in a tree*). Teach the word *gum tree* (an Australian tree with a sticky sap called 'gum', which the kookaburra is eating in the picture). Show pupils the gum drops you have brought and say they have the same name. Say *Who are his friends?* (*monkeys*).

8 Say *Now listen to the song and put a number by the pictures.* Play the recording. Pupils number the pictures 1 to 3. Check by calling out the key words from each verse.
Key (from left to right) 2 eating/gum drop; 3 counting/monkeys; 1 king/laugh

Step 2

1 If necessary, remind pupils about the kookaburra. Say *Is the kookaburra happy or sad? Where does he live? Who are his friends? What does he eat?*

2 If necessary, give each pupil their own worksheet 1. Pupils read the words in the word box. Explain vocabulary as necessary. Pupils guess where the words go in the song. Then they listen and write them in.
Key 1 gum tree, 2 bush, 3 Eating, 4 there, 5 Kookaburra, 6 monkeys

3 Practise any new words. Show pupils how to frown and wag their fingers crossly for *Stop, Kookaburra!* and *Hey, Kookaburra!* Say *Who says 'That one's not a monkey – that one's me!'* (*boy in picture 3*).

4 Say *Now let's sing the song.* Play the recording. Pupils sing together and do the actions.

5 If time, pupils colour the pictures and eat the gum drops you have brought!

Step 3

1 Give each pupil worksheet 2. Stick the A3 copy on the board. Elicit the names of the Australian animals on the fact cards (*crocodile, emu, koala* and *kangaroo*).

2 Ask questions about the animals, including all the animals and the facts on the worksheet e.g. *What's this? Has it got a long tail? What's the name of this bird? Can it fly?* (*No*).

3 Show pupils the missing sentences. Say *Now read and match.* Pupils do this individually or in pairs, choosing and copying the correct sentences. Check.
Key crocodile 2, 8, 11; koala 3, 5, 9; emu 1, 6, 10; kangaroo 4, 7, 12

4 Ask questions e.g. *Can a kangaroo swim? Can a crocodile climb trees?*

1 Listen to the song and number the pictures.

2 Write in the words.

| monkeys | there | ~~gum tree~~ | Kookaburra | bush | Eating |

Kookaburra sits in the old (1) ...gum tree... ,

Merry, merry king of the (2) .... is he.

Laugh, Kookaburra! Laugh Kookaburra!

Great your life must be.

Kookaburra sits in the old gum tree,

(3) .... all the gum drops he can see.

Stop, Kookaburra! Stop, Kookaburra!

Leave some (4) .... for me!

(5) .... sits in the old gum tree,

Counting all the (6) .... he can see.

Hey, Kookaburra! Hey!

That one's not a monkey, that one's me!

Read and match the sentences about these Australian animals.

crocodile

It's got a long tail. ....

....

....

koala

It's got a black nose. ....

....

....

emu

It can't fly. ....

....

....

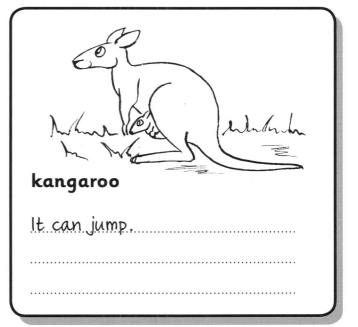

kangaroo

It can jump. ....

....

....

1 ~~It can't fly.~~

2 ~~It's got a long tail.~~

3 ~~It's got a black nose.~~

4 ~~It can jump.~~

5 It can climb trees.

6 Its neck is blue.

7 It carries its babies inside it.

8 It lives near water. It can swim.

9 It's small and grey.

10 It can run fast.

11 It's green and brown.

12 It's got big, brown feet.

This old man

LANGUAGE FOCUS
words which rhyme with numbers *1–10*
'pet' words

LEVEL 2

AGE RANGE 8–10

TIME
Step 1: 20 minutes
Step 2: 20 minutes
Step 3: 15 minutes

MATERIALS
Lyrics p.133

Step 1
Worksheet 1 for each pupil plus 1 x A3 copy

Step 2
Flashcards for 'number words' *one* to *ten*, worksheet 1 for each pupil plus 1 x A3 copy

Step 3
Worksheet 2 for each pupil plus 1 x A3 copy

FOLLOW-UP ACTIVITIES
Pupils find words which rhyme with colours

Class project on how to look after pets (p.16)

Step 1 Matching pictures with numbers *1–10*, listening to the song, making up rhyming sentences
Step 2 Following rhyming words in a word maze, singing the song
Step 3 Reading about pets, doing a pets survey

Step 1

1 Count with pupils up to ten. Draw a sun on the board and say *Listen. Sun.* Drill. Then say *Listen. One. Sun. Sun rhymes with one.* Say *What rhymes with two?* Elicit *shoe.* Say *One, sun. Two, shoe. Let's listen to a song about number rhymes.*

2 Stick the A3 copy of worksheet 1 on the board and give each pupil a copy. Teach any unknown vocabulary from the pictures and drill. Point out the example. In pairs, pupils discuss which numbers and pictures match.

3 Play the recording. Pupils listen to the song and draw lines. Check. Confirm the last three numbers and their rhyming words.
Key 1 sun, 2 shoe, 3 tree, 4 door, 5 hive, 6 sticks, 7 eleven, 8 gate, 9 line, 10 pen

4 Elicit other words that rhyme with numbers e.g. *one – run, fun; two – blue, zoo,* etc. Write them on the board. Say *Now let's make rhymes.* Give examples first e.g. *I like to run. It's fun. I lost my shoe. It was blue.*

Step 2

1 Write the numbers 1–10 on the board. Show the flashcards of 'number words' in order. Get pupils to read them aloud. Then get pupils to stick them next to the figures on the board.

2 Remind pupils of the song and elicit the rhyming words *one/sun, two/shoe,* etc.

3 If necessary, give each pupil their worksheet 1 and stick the A3 copy on the board. Point to the bottom of the sheet. Ask questions to establish that the dog is waiting for his bone while the old man, his master, is lost and is *rolling home* i.e. not going in a straight line.

4 Say *Let's help the old man find the dog!* Show the linked example *one* and *sun* in the maze. Say *What's next?* Pupils find the word *two* and draw a line. Pupils work in pairs, linking the rhyming words.
Key see 3 in Step 1 above

5 Play the recording for pupils to check, then ask them to read the words in the correct order.

6 Pupils draw the bone in the dog's mouth. Teach pupils verse 1 of the song. Then sing the song, following the words in the maze.

Step 3

1 If necessary, remind pupils of the old man's dog. Elicit other types of pets.

2 Give each pupil worksheet 2 and stick the A3 copy on the board. Teach/Review vocabulary for the pets on the worksheet (*cat, fish, rabbit, hamster*).

3 Check vocabulary in the speech bubbles. Then say *Match the children and their pets.* Pupils draw lines. Check.
Key 1e, 2b, 3d, 4a, 5c

4 Talk about the different pets. Say *What do they eat? Where do they live or sleep?* etc.

5 Say *We're going to find out about the pets in our class.* Pupils work in groups of four and write their names in the 'Name' column. They write two more types of pets in the last two columns.

6 Pupils complete the chart by asking each other e.g. *How many dogs have you got?* and recording the numbers on the chart.

7 Pupils feed back to the class the most popular type of pet in their group.

This old man 1

1 Match the numbers with the things that rhyme.

2 Join the rhyming words and help the old man find his dog.

START

one	fine	sure	sheep	kite	ball	train
show	sun	shoe	her	red	you	eleven
toe	two	three	robot	pen	carrot	run
know	tree	thing	green	ruler	meet	goat
fur	four	our	dog	kite	eight	gate
your	poor	door	ever	eleven	never	nine
mine	socks	five	sacks	seven	phone	line
live	hive	six	sticks	even	ten	pen

WAY HOME

1 Read and match the children and their pets.

1 My pet eats meat.
It sleeps in a basket.
It likes going for walks.

2 My pet eats meat and fish. It sleeps on my bed. It likes catching mice.

3 My pet lives in a tank.
It likes swimming.

4 My pet lives in a hutch. It eats grass and vegetables. It likes digging.

5 My pet lives in a cage. It eats nuts and vegetables. It likes running on its wheel.

a rabbit

b cat

c hamster

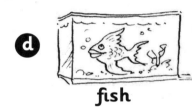

d fish

e dog

2 Ask your friends *How many pets have you got?* Which pets are most popular?

Name	Dog	Cat	Fish	Rabbit	Hamster		

We've got the whole world in our hands

LANGUAGE FOCUS
people close to us
nature
towns and cities
rubbish and recycling

LEVEL 2

AGE RANGE 8–10

TIME
Step 1: 25 minutes
Step 2: 20 minutes
Step 3: 20 minutes

MATERIALS
⊙117 Lyrics p.133

Step 1
Globe or picture of Earth, flashcards of blown-up pictures from worksheet 1, worksheet 1 for each pupil

Step 2
Worksheet 1 for each pupil

Step 3
Postcards or magazine pictures of beautiful places in the world, items of clean rubbish, worksheet 2 for each pupil plus 1 x A3 copy

FOLLOW-UP ACTIVITIES
Class project on beautiful places in the world (p.16)

Pupils keep a 'recycling' diary for two days (p.16)

Step 1 Gap-filling the things in the world, listening to the song
Step 2 Ordering pictures, singing the song, discussing what's important in the world, (drawing)
Step 3 Matching 'recycling' texts to pictures, categorising rubbish

Step 1

1 Hold up a globe or picture of the Earth and say *What's this?* Elicit *the earth* or *the world*. Say *Yes, I've got the whole world in my hands.*

2 Elicit important things in the world. Say *What people do you love in the world?* Draw/use flashcards to elicit *parents, mother, father, brothers, sisters, friends, family*. Write them on the board.

3 Say *What can we see in the sky?* Draw/use flashcards to elicit *sun, moon, stars, rain, wind* and *clouds.* Say *What water is there in the world?* Elicit *rivers, seas, oceans.* Say *Where do we live in the world?* Elicit *towns, mountains* and *cities.* Write all words on the board.

4 Say *Listen to the song 'We've got the whole world in our hands'. Which words can you hear?* Play the recording. Pupils circle the words on the board that are in the song.

5 Give worksheet 1 to each pupil. They look at the pictures and read the words. Pupils work in pairs to fill in the gaps from the word box. Check by playing the recording again.
Key (from left to right) world, sisters, family, moon, rain, people, clouds, mountains, cities, seas

Step 2

1 Write the letters *W, H, B, S, F, P, R, M, C, O, T* on the board. In pairs, pupils write down any things from the song that begin with these letters. (*W – world, wind, whole; H – hands; B – brothers; S – sisters, sun, stars, seas; F – friends, family; P – people; R - rain, rivers; M – mountains, moon; C – clouds, cities; O – oceans; T – towns*). Elicit ideas.

2 If necessary, give each pupil worksheet 1. Say *Listen to the song and put the pictures in order.* Play the recording. Pupils listen and draw lines between the pictures. **Key** see song lyrics p.133 Check, then say *Now let's sing the song.* Pupils sing the song, using the worksheet to help.

3 Discuss with pupils the things in the world that are important to them.

4 If time, pupils draw themselves with the 'people everywhere' on the worksheet.

Step 3

1 Show postcards or pictures of beautiful places in the world. Elicit other examples.

2 Remind pupils of the title of the song. Explain this means we must look after the world.

3 Give worksheet 2 to each pupil and stick the A3 copy on the board. Elicit/Teach the words *dirty* and *rubbish* from the picture of the landfill site and *recycle* from the picture of the girl.

4 Pupils read the sentences and number the pictures. Check and help with vocabulary.
Key 2 (top right-hand), 1 (bottom left-hand), 3 (bottom right-hand)

5 Say *What can we do with our rubbish?* (*Recycle it!*) Use the rubbish you have brought or the worksheet to teach the different recycling categories. Elicit/Teach *plastic, glass, paper, clothes, food* and *metal*.

6 Look at the picture of the picnic table at the bottom of worksheet 2. Say *Let's clean the picnic up and recycle the rubbish.* Pupils circle all the rubbish they can see in the picture and then draw it in the correct recycling bin. Use the A3 copy of worksheet 2 to check.
Key glass – bottle; plastic – yoghurt pot; clothes – shoe; food – sandwich; paper – magazine; metal – drinks can

1 Write the words from the song. Then listen and draw lines to order the pictures.

| cities | moon | ~~world~~ | mountains | sisters | seas |
| family | clouds | people | rain | | |

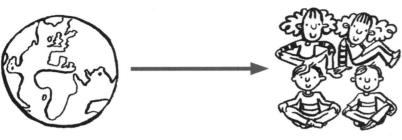

the whole
world

brothers and
....

friends and
....

....
and stars

sun and
....

....
everywhere

wind and
....

rivers and
....

....
and oceans

towns and
....

1   Read and match the words and pictures.

1   The world is beautiful. We must look after it.

2   We don't want a dirty world. We mustn't put rubbish under the ground.

3   Don't throw your rubbish away. Recycle it!

2   Find and circle the rubbish. Then draw it in the correct recycling bin.

glass   plastic   metal   paper   clothes   food

Primary Music Box

Do your ears hang low?

LANGUAGE FOCUS
parts of the body, actions
can for ability

LEVEL 2

AGE RANGE 8–10

TIME
Step 1: 25 minutes
Step 2: 15 minutes
Step 3: 20 minutes

MATERIALS
◉ 118 Lyrics p.134

Step 1
Worksheet 1 for each pupil
plus flashcards of blown-up
copies of the four pictures

Step 2
Worksheet 1 for each pupil

Step 3
Worksheet 2 cut into
individual cards; one set for
each group of seven or eight
pupils

FOLLOW-UP ACTIVITIES
Pupils make up *Can you ... ?*
questions for the class

Pupils have a talent show,
showing the class other
unusual or talented things
they can do (p.16)

Step 1 Reviewing/Learning 'action' vocabulary, listening to the song and ordering pictures and sentences
Step 2 Learning verses 2, 3 and 4, singing the song
Step 3 Playing *Can you ... ?*

Step 1

1 Get pupils to stand up. Demonstrate and say *Can you touch your toes?* Then say *Can you stand on one leg? Can you wiggle your toes?* Demonstrate both actions and ask pupils to copy. Say *Can you wiggle your ears?* If any pupils can do this, get them to show the class.

2 Say *We're going to listen to a funny song.* Give worksheet 1 to each pupil. Get pupils to look at the pictures and the question under each one. Pupils fill in the gaps with words from the word box.
Key nose, tongue, eyes, ears

3 Say *Listen to the song and number the pictures.* Play the recording. Pupils listen and order the verse pictures from 1 to 4.
Key 1 ears, 2 tongue, 3 nose, 4 eyes

4 Use flashcards and actions to teach *hang low/down, wobble, wiggle to and fro, tie in a knot/bow, flap up and down, fly around the town, pop out, flop, bounce.*

5 Pupils look at the jumbled lines from verse 1 of the song. Read the lines aloud, explaining vocabulary as necessary.

6 Say *Listen and number the lines.* Play verse 1. Pupils order the lines 1 to 7. Check.
Key in order from left to right 3, 5, 6, 1/7, 4, 7/1, 2

7 Play verse 1 of the song again while pupils do the actions.

Step 2

1 Call out instructions from the song e.g. *Tie your ears in a bow. Bounce your eyes up and down.* Pupils do the actions.

2 If necessary, give worksheet 1 to each pupil. Pupils read out the lines of verse 1 in the correct order. Say *Now let's sing verse 1 together.* Play verse 1. Pupils sing and do the actions.

3 Say *Can you remember the other verses from the song?* Look at the pictures again. Try to elicit the first two lines from each verse.
Key see song lyrics p.134.
Play the recording of verses 2, 3 and 4, pausing as necessary for pupils to drill the lines. Point out that after the first two lines of each verse the other words are repeated each time.

4 Say *Let's sing the whole song together.* Play the recording. Pupils sing, using the worksheet to help them and doing the actions.

Step 3

1 Play Simon Says to review/teach *wiggle, touch, stand on one leg, click your fingers, walk backwards, hop, turn around, close your eyes, fold your arms.*

2 Say *We're going to find out who can do the most funny things.* Write *Can you cross your eyes?* on the board. Drill the question and the answers *Yes I can / No I can't.* Pupils ask their partner, who replies and demonstrates whether he/she can do the action or not.

3 Put pupils into groups of seven or eight. Give each group a set of cut-out cards from worksheet 2 to share out. Pupils work in their groups, asking the questions on their cards. Help with pronunciation. Each group counts how many of them can do the different actions and writes the number on the card.

4 Groups report back e.g. *Five people can walk backwards* and pupils demonstrate.

Do your ears hang low? 1

1   Write the words. Then listen and number the pictures.

| eyes   tongue   ears   nose |

Does your .... hang low? ☐   Does your .... hang down? ☐

Do your .... pop out? ☐   Do your .... hang low? ☐

2   Listen and number the lines from the song.

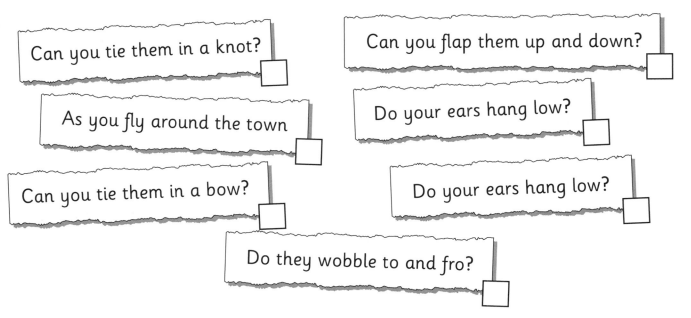

Can you tie them in a knot? ☐

Can you flap them up and down? ☐

As you fly around the town ☐

Do your ears hang low? ☐

Can you tie them in a bow? ☐

Do your ears hang low? ☐

Do they wobble to and fro? ☐

Ask your friends *Can you ... ?*

Can you wiggle
your ears?

Can you wiggle
your nose?

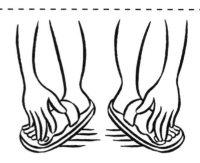

Can you touch
your toes?

Can you wiggle
your toes?

Can you click your
fingers?

Can you walk
backwards?

Can you hop on
one leg?

Can you turn around
with your eyes closed?

Can you touch your
knees with your nose?

Can you touch your nose
with your tongue?

Can you fold your arms
behind your back?

Can you stand on one leg
with your eyes closed?

I found a peanut

2.6

LANGUAGE FOCUS
food and food hygiene
past simple tense and
question forms

LEVEL 2

AGE RANGE 8–10

TIME
Step 1: 20 minutes
Step 2: 20 minutes
Step 3: 20 minutes

MATERIALS
⊙ 119 Lyrics p.134

Step 1
Food items (hidden in
classroom), packet of
peanuts, in shells if possible
(make sure no pupils have nut
allergies)

Step 2
Worksheet 1 for each pupil

Step 3
Worksheet 2 for each pupil
plus 1 x A3 copy

**FOLLOW-UP
ACTIVITIES**
Class make up a new version
of the song with different
answers to the questions
(p.14)

Pupils create a food safety
poster with Dos and Don'ts
(p.16)

Step 1 Learning/Reviewing food vocabulary, listening to the song, discussing food safety
Step 2 Matching questions and answers, singing the song
Step 3 Reading a shopping list, searching for 'food' items in a picture

---

Step 1

1 Before class, hide some things, plus food from worksheet 2 in the classroom e.g. a red pencil, a coin, an apple, a banana, etc. Say *Some things are hiding in this classroom. Can you find an apple? Can you find a coin?* etc. Pupils find them.

2 Say *A girl found some food in the street. What was it, do you think?* Pupils guess. Write suggestions on the board.

3 Say *Listen. What did the girl find?* Play verse 1. Elicit and write *peanut* on the board and explain if necessary or show the peanuts you have brought.

4 Say *Where did she find the peanut?* Elicit possible answers. Write them on the board. Make sure *in a dustbin* is on the list.

5 Say *Let's listen and find out.* Play verses 1–5. Pupils listen. Elicit (*in a dustbin*). Say *What did she do with the peanut?* (*She ate it*). Elicit other information that pupils understood.

6 Say *Is it good to eat food from a dustbin? Why not?* Elicit other ideas about food hygiene generally e.g. *don't eat food from dirty plates/off the floor, wash your hands, wash fruit and vegetables, put food in the fridge, don't put food in the sun*, etc.

Step 2

1 If necessary, remind pupils of the song. Say *What did the girl find?* (*a peanut*). *Where did she find it?* (*in a dustbin*).

2 Give each pupil worksheet 1. Read questions 1–7. Check comprehension.

3 Teach/Review *disgusting, cut, open, called* (*phoned*), *doctor*. Pupils read the answers with pictures on the right of the worksheet and try to match them to the questions.

4 Say *Now let's listen to the song for the questions and answers.* Play the recording, pausing as necessary. Check by asking the questions and eliciting the correct answers.
Key 1d, 2e, 3c, 4a, 5f, 6b, 7g

5 Drill questions and answers, then do a cross-class chant: one half of the class asking the questions and the other replying.

6 Say *Now let's sing the song.* Play the recording. Pupils sing, using the worksheet to help them.

Step 3

1 If necessary, remind pupils of the song and say *Where can you buy peanuts?* (*in a shop/ supermarket*). Say *What other food and fruit can you buy in a shop/supermarket?* Elicit food words and write them on the board.

2 Give each pupil worksheet 2. Point to the shopping list. Say *Today you're going shopping.* Teach/Review any new words as necessary.

3 Read the first two items on the shopping list (*1 sandwich/2 fish*). Say *Can you find the sandwich and the two fish in the shop?* Pupils find the circled examples.

4 Set a time limit of five to ten minutes for pupils to work in pairs and search in the picture for the other shopping list items. (They are not always together!)

5 Use the A3 copy of worksheet 2 to check.

6 If time, pupils can draw their favourite food on the top shelf above the cakes.

Listen and match the questions and answers.

1 What did you find?

a It was disgusting!

2 Where did you find it?

b He cut me open.

3 What did you do with it?

c Well, I ate it.

4 What did it taste like?

d I found a peanut.

5 What did you do then?

e In a dustbin.

6 What did the doctor do?

f I called the doctor.

7 What did he find there?

g He found a peanut ...

Read the shopping list. Find and circle the food in the picture.

Shopping list

1 sandwich

2 fish

4 cakes

3 bananas

5 apples

3 onions

2 carrots

5 sweets

4 cherries

1 peanut

She'll be coming round the mountain

LANGUAGE FOCUS

She'll ... , She'll be ... ing
going to future
question words *How, What, Where, Who*
words linked to American culture

LEVEL 2

AGE RANGE 8–10

TIME

Step 1: 20 minutes
Step 2: 25 minutes
Step 3: 20 minutes

MATERIALS

◎ 🎵120 Lyrics p.135

Step 1
Worksheet 1 for each pupil plus 1 x A3 copy, colouring pencils

Step 2
Worksheet 1 for each pupil plus 1 x A3 copy

Step 3
Map of the world or globe, worksheet 2 for each pair or group of pupils

FOLLOW-UP ACTIVITIES

Pupils make up new verses for the song (p.14)

Pupils write a quiz about a different country (p.17)

Step 1 Thinking about visitors, listening to the song and ordering pictures, learning the chorus
Step 2 Gap-filling and singing the song with actions
Step 3 Doing a quiz on North American culture

Step 1

1 Say *Someone is going to visit your family.* Elicit ideas by asking *Who's going to come? How are they going to travel? What are they going to wear? Where are they going to sleep? What are you all going to eat?*

2 Give each pupil worksheet 1 and stick the A3 copy on the board. Pupils look at the first picture of the family. Say *Are they happy or sad?* (happy). Say *Someone is going to visit them. It's a woman. Who is it?* Pupils guess; there is no answer in the song.

3 Using the other pictures, elicit/teach vocabulary e.g. *Where is she going to come from?* (the mountain), *What is she going to drive?* (carriage with horses), *Where is she going to sleep?* (in Grandma's bed), *What are they going to eat?* (bananas), *What is she going to wear?* (pyjamas).

4 Point to the picture numbered 1. Say *Listen to the song and write numbers by the other pictures.* Play the recording. Pupils write in the numbers of the pictures. Check. **Key** 1, 4, 5, 3, 2

5 Say *Listen. The family are very happy. What are they saying?* Play the chorus of the song. Elicit and drill *Aye aye yippy yippy aye.* Play the chorus again. Pupils sing the chorus and clap.

6 Get pupils to draw the visitor in the empty box on the worksheet and colour the pictures.

Step 2

1 If necessary, give out worksheet 1 again. Say *Which country do the family come from?* (the USA). Explain the American phrase *Yee hah!* (when riding a horse).

2 Play the recording, miming and saying the interjections in each verse. Then say them in random order and get pupils to do the actions.
   • *Toot toot!* (pretend to squeeze a car horn)
   • *Yee hah!* (pretend to ride a horse)
   • *Lovely!* (clasp your hands in admiration)
   • *Snore snore!*
   • *Yum yum!* (rub your tummy)

3 Use the A3 copy to show pupils the song words on worksheet 1 and the words in the box. Read each line, pausing at the gaps each time. Elicit the missing words by referring to the pictures. Give time for pupils to write them in. **Key** 1 mountain/toot!, 2 horses/Yee hah!, 3 pyjamas/Lovely!, 4 Grandma/snore!, 5 bananas/yum! Play the song again to check.

4 Say *Now let's sing the song.* Play the recording. Pupils sing the song and act out the interjections.

Step 3

1 If necessary, remind pupils that the song is from the USA and find it on a map or globe.

2 Elicit what pupils already know about the USA, e.g. *What are the names of the cities? What animals can you see there? What famous people are American?*

3 Say *Let's answer some questions about the USA.* Put pupils into pairs/groups. Give each pair/group worksheet 2. Read through the questions to check comprehension. Pupils read and answer the questions, then exchange worksheets with another pair/group. Read out the correct answers. Pupils mark each other's worksheets. **Key** 1c, 2c, 3a, 4b, 5c, 6a, 7c, 8b, 9a

4 If time, pairs/groups make up their own 'USA' question for the rest of the class e.g. about TV, food, towns or places.

1   Listen and number the pictures. Draw the visitor.

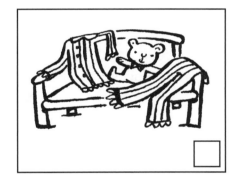

2   Choose and write the words from the song.

bananas	mountain	Grandma	horses	pyjamas
snore!	toot!	Yee hah!	yum!	Lovely!

1   She'll be coming round the .... when she comes. Toot ....

2   She'll be driving six white .... when she comes. ....

3   She'll be wearing pink .... when she comes. ....

4   She will have to sleep with .... when she comes. Snore, ...

5   We will all have some .... when she comes. Yum ....

What do you know about the USA?

1 How many states are in the United States of America (USA)?

a) 48
b) 50
c) 52

2 Which is the flag of the USA?

a) b) c)
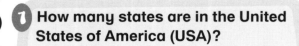

3 Which is a typical animal from the USA?

a) b) c)
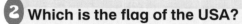

bald eagle   kangaroo   panda

4 Which monument can you see near New York?

a) b) c)

Eiffel Tower   Statue of   Taj Mahal
            Liberty

5 What is the money of the USA?

a) Pounds

       b) Euros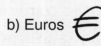

c) Dollars

6 What sport is most popular in the USA?

a)   b)   c)
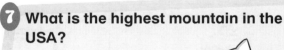

baseball   cricket   bowling

7 What is the highest mountain in the USA?

a) Mount Everest
b) Mont Blanc
c) Mount McKinley

8 Who was the first American president?

a)

Abraham Lincoln

b)

George Washington

c)

Barack Obama

9 What food is typically American?

a)

hamburgers   b)

rice

c)

spaghetti

The animals went in two by two

2.8

Step 1 Learning/Reviewing animal vocabulary, listening to the song and ticking pictures

Step 2 Matching rhyming lines, singing the song

Step 3 Classifying animals into different types, making a Tree of Life

LANGUAGE FOCUS
animals and animal categories
rhyming words

LEVEL 2

AGE RANGE 8–10

TIME
Step 1: 25 minutes
Step 2: 20 minutes
Step 3: 25 minutes

MATERIALS
🔘 **T21** Lyrics p.135

Step 1
Worksheet 1 for each pupil plus 1 x A3 copy, pieces of paper, each with the name of an animal from the Ark, (colouring pencils)

Step 2
Worksheet 1 for each pupil

Step 3
Worksheet 2 for each pupil plus 1 x A3 copy

FOLLOW-UP ACTIVITIES
Class make a Tree of Life animal poster with pictures of their favourite animals (p.16)

Pupils design a luxury ark (p.17)

Step 1

1 Use an outline of an ark on the board to teach/elicit *ark*. Say *Do you know the story of the Ark?* Explain the story if necessary (see Resource bank p.14). Elicit what animals pupils think were in the Ark and write them on the board.

2 Stick the A3 copy of worksheet 1 on the board and give each pupil a copy. Pupils check which animals listed on the board are in the picture. Elicit/Teach the remainder.

3 Say *Listen to the song and tick the animals you hear.* Play the recording. Say *Which animal isn't in the song?* (*giraffe*). Ask pupils which animals they would save from the flood.

4 Give a pupil a secret animal name to mime for the class to guess, or play as a team game.

5 If time, pupils can decorate the Ark and colour the animals on it.

Step 2

1 If necessary, give pupils two minutes to write down any animals they remember from the song. Play the recording for them to check.

2 If necessary, give each pupil worksheet 1 again. Read the sentences at the bottom and check comprehension. Show the example and how the lines rhyme e.g. *two, kangaroo*. Say *Now listen to the song and find the rhymes.* Play the recording, pausing as necessary.
Key 1c, 2f, 3i, 4g, 5a, 6d, 7h, 8b, 9e

3 Practise pronunciation. Say *Now let's sing the song.* Play the recording. Pupils sing, using the worksheet to help.

4 Discuss the ideas in the song *Why does the hippo get stuck in the door?* (*she's very fat*), *Why is the turtle late?* (*he's very slow*), *Why does the monkey do tricks?* (*he's naughty*), etc.

Step 3

1 Say *We're going to look at families of animals.* Stick the A3 copy of worksheet 2 on the board and give a copy to each pupil. Show pupils the two main groups; *vertebrates* (point to your own, or draw, a spine) and *arthropods* (no spine) e.g. insects.

2 Follow the branches above *vertebrates* and find the 'monkey' picture for *mammals*. Say *Where do monkeys live?* (*on land*). *Do they have eggs or babies?* (*babies*). Point out the word box. Say *Look at the names of the animals in the Ark. Which ones are mammals?* (*monkey, elephant, giraffe, kangaroo, hippopotamus*). Pupils copy the names into the *mammals* branch of the tree.

3 For *birds, reptiles, fish* and *amphibians*, use the pictures on the tree to discuss the identifying features e.g. *birds – have feathers, most can fly, lay eggs, have two legs; reptiles – scaly skin and claws, lay hard eggs on land, have cold blood; fish – live in water, swim, lay eggs, no arms or legs* and *amphibians – can live in or out of water, soft skin, lay soft eggs in water, have no claws, cold-blooded.*

4 In pairs, pupils write the words in the word box on the correct tree branch. Check.
Key birds (hen only), reptiles (crocodile, turtle), fish (none in song) and amphibians (frog only)

5 Remind pupils of the meaning of *arthropod*. Say *What insects are in the song?* (*wasp, ant, bumblebee*). Spiders and crabs are also arthropods.

6 Complete the tree, eliciting one more example for each category.

The animals went in two by two 1

1 Listen and tick (✓) the animals in the song.

2 Read and match the lines of the song.

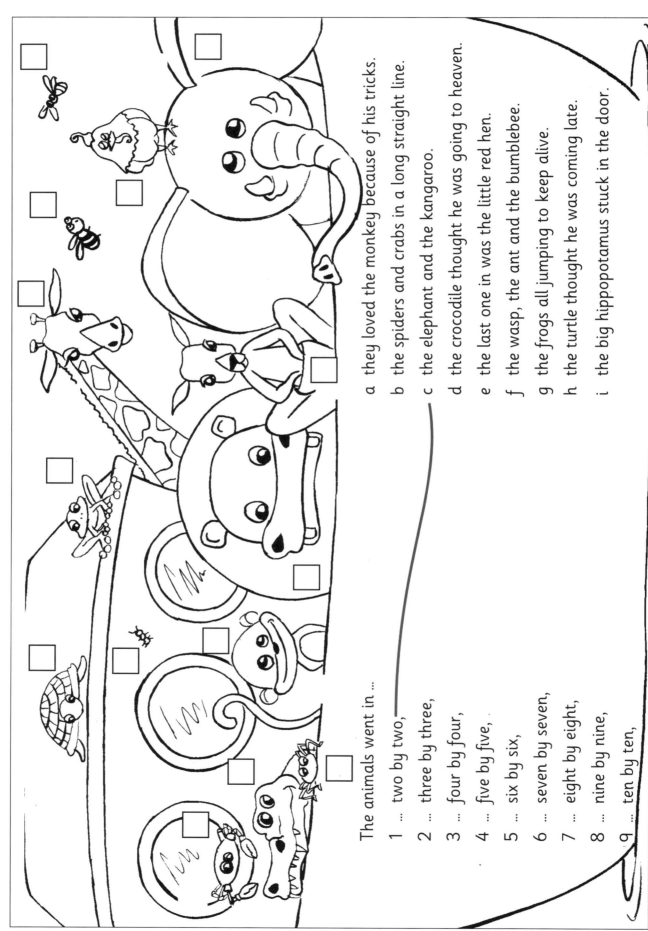

a they loved the monkey because of his tricks.

b the spiders and crabs in a long straight line.

c the elephant and the kangaroo.

d the crocodile thought he was going to heaven.

e the last one in was the little red hen.

f the wasp, the ant and the bumblebee.

g the frogs all jumping to keep alive.

h the turtle thought he was coming late.

i the big hippopotamus stuck in the door.

The animals went in ...

1 ... two by two,

2 ... three by three,

3 ... four by four,

4 ... five by five,

5 ... six by six,

6 ... seven by seven,

7 ... eight by eight,

8 ... nine by nine,

9 ... ten by ten,

The animals went in two by two 2

Put the animals in their place on the Tree of Life.

> elephant   crocodile   wasp   ~~frog~~   hippopotamus   ~~turtle~~
> ~~hen~~   kangaroo   ~~ant~~   crab   bumblebee   ~~monkey~~
> spider   ~~fish~~   giraffe

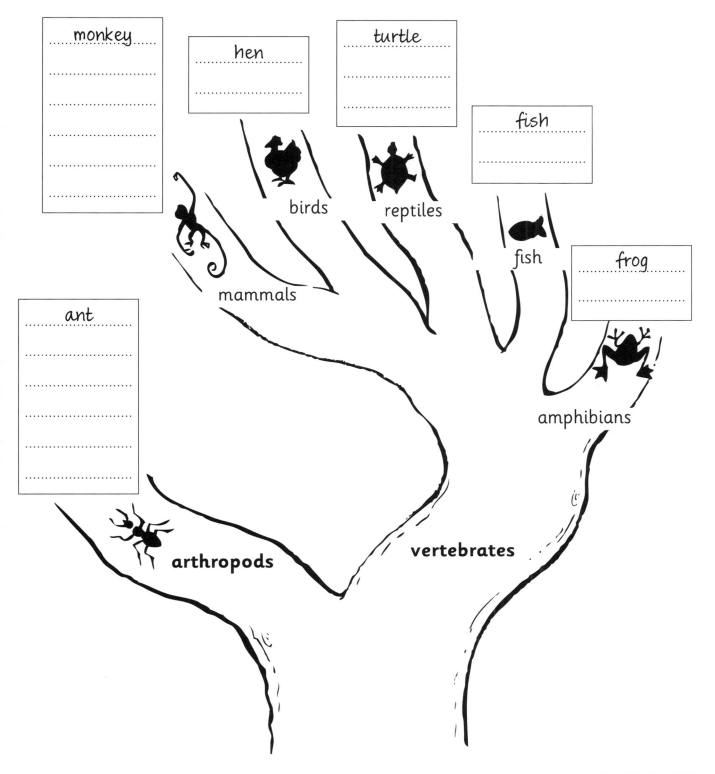

2.9

Jingle bells

LANGUAGE FOCUS
seasonal activities and weather
'Christmas' words
instructions

LEVEL 2

AGE RANGE 8–10

TIME
Step 1: 15 minutes
Step 2: 20 minutes
Step 3: 25 minutes

MATERIALS
🔘 122 Lyrics p.136

Step 1
Worksheet 1 for each pupil plus 1 x A3 copy

Step 2
Worksheet 1 for each pupil

Step 3
Ready-made pop-up sleigh card, worksheet 2 for each pupil, 19cm x 19cm card, scissors, glue, colouring pencils

FOLLOW-UP ACTIVITIES
Groups of four pupils each draw a picture for one season, then combine them into a 'year' poster (p.16)

Pupils make words from the word 'Christmastime'

Step 1	Learning/Reviewing 'seasons/weather' lexis, listening to the song and pointing
Step 2	Choosing the correct words and singing the song, drawing a self-portrait doing a winter activity
Step 3	Making a pop-up Christmas card

Step 1

1 Say *What's the weather like today?* Elicit/Teach weather words as appropriate and draw the symbols on the board. Elicit and teach all the seasons.

2 Point to the word *winter*. Say *What's the weather like in winter?* Elicit/Teach *It's rainy, It's foggy, It's snowy, It's windy, It's cold, It's cloudy.*

3 Stick the A3 copy of worksheet 1 on the board and give each pupil a copy. Say *What's the season in this picture?* (*winter*). *What's the weather like?* (*snowy*). *Are the people happy?* (*Yes*).

4 Use the picture to pre-teach vocabulary from the song e.g. *What are the people in?* Teach *sleigh. What animal can you see?* (*a horse*). *What are the people doing?* (*riding in a sleigh / laughing*). *Are they in the town or countryside?* (*the countryside*). Point to and elicit the word *fields*. Say *What can you see on the horse's tail?* (*bells*).

5 Play the introduction to the song only (with the jingling bells) and teach the word *jingle*. Say *We're going to listen to a song called Jingle bells. It's about riding in this sleigh.* Play the recording. Get pupils to point to the things in the picture as they hear them mentioned in the song. (*snow, horse, sleigh, fields, bells, tail,* etc.)

Step 2

1 If necessary, remind pupils of the song by miming and eliciting *Jingle bells.* Give worksheet 1 to each pupil.

2 Point out the song text and the alternative pairs of words. Say *Listen and circle the words in the song.* Play the recording, pausing as necessary. Check.
Key 1 snow, 2 horse, 3 Laughing, 4 Bells, 5 sing, 6 jingle, 7 ride

3 Explain other words and drill as necessary, (*dashing, bobtail, making spirits bright*) using the picture or mime and gesture. Say *Let's sing the song together.* Play the recording.

4 Say *In the snow, you can ride in a sleigh. What other things can you do?* Elicit e.g. *build a snowman, go skiing, throw snowballs, go skating.* Pupils draw a picture of themselves doing one of these activities in the space in the picture.

5 Pupils show their pictures and say what they like doing e.g. *I like building a snowman.*

Step 3

1 Say *What do people send at Christmas time?* (*Christmas cards*). Say *We're going to make a card with a picture inside it. Who uses a sleigh at Christmas time?* Elicit/Teach *Father Christmas.* Say *What does he have on his sleigh?* (*Christmas presents*). Show pupils your ready-made sleigh card and say *We're going to make a card like this.*

2 Give each pupil worksheet 2 and a piece of card. Use the pictures on the worksheet to show how to make the card.

3 Say *What do you write on a Christmas card?* Write *Happy/Merry Christmas* or *Season's Greetings* on the board for pupils to copy onto their card. Pupils write *To … , With love from …* on the front of the card, decorate it and take it home.

1 Listen to the song and point to the things in the picture.

2 Listen and circle the words in the song.

Dashing through the (1) *ice / snow*,

In a one (2) *horse / cow* open sleigh,

Over fields we go,

(3) *Laughing / Singing* all the way.

(4) *Stars / Bells* on bobtail ring,

Making spirits bright.

What fun it is to laugh and (5) *play / sing*

A sleighing song tonight.

Oh, jingle bells, (6) *bringing / jingle bells*,

Jingle all the way.

Oh what fun it is to (7) *ride / sit*

In a one-horse open sleigh. Hey!

3 Draw yourself in the picture.

Make a pop-up Christmas card.

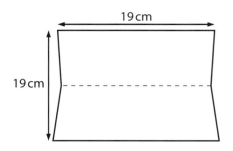

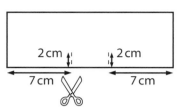

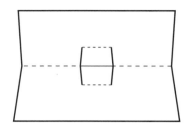

Take a piece of card 19x19cms and fold it down the centre.

Make two 2cm cuts, 7cms from each end of the fold.

Open the card and push out the little box that you have made.

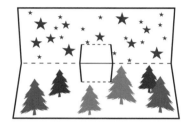

Colour in a starry sky and trees.

Cut out Father Christmas and his sleigh and colour them.

Stick Father Christmas in his sleigh onto the front of the little box.

Write your Christmas message.

Michael Finnegan

2.10

LANGUAGE FOCUS
irregular past tenses
prepositions
opposites
board game instructions

LEVEL 2

AGE RANGE 8–10

TIME

Step 1: 20 minutes
Step 2: 15 minutes
Step 3: 20 minutes

MATERIALS

🔘123 Lyrics p.136

Step 1
A piece of paper for each
pupil, worksheet 1 for each
pupil

Step 2
Worksheet 1 for each pupil

Step 3
Worksheet 2 for each pair
of pupils plus 1 x A3 copy,
a coin for each pair/small
group of pupils to play the
game

FOLLOW-UP ACTIVITIES

Class sing the song faster and
faster (p.13)

Play Simon Says where pupils
do the opposite of what you
say (p.15)

Step 1 Listening to the song, drawing a picture of Michael Finnegan, ordering lines from the song

Step 2 Singing the song, doing an opposites matching activity

Step 3 Playing a 'Michael Finnegan' board game

Step 1

1 Say *We're going to listen to a song about a funny man. What's his name? Listen carefully and find out.* Play verse 1 and then ask *What's his name?* (*Michael Finnegan*).

2 Then say *Now listen again and tell me what he looks like. Is he old or young? Has he got a beard?* Pre-teach the words *chin* and *whiskers* from the song. Then play verse 1 of the recording and elicit the answers (*old*) (*Yes and no!*).

3 Now play verse 2 and ask *What did Michael Finnegan catch?* (*a fish*). Then play the last verse of the song and ask *Is he fat or thin?* (*fat and thin!*).

4 Ask *Who can draw Michael Finnegan?* Pupils draw what they think he looks like.

5 Give out worksheet 1. Pupils look at the pictures of Michael Finnegan at the top of the worksheet and compare these with their own.

6 Then read the song lines with the pupils. Explain that *chinnegan* and *pinnegan* (for *chin* and *pin*) are made up to rhyme with *Finnegan*. Say *Now listen to the song again and number the sentences.* Play the recording twice for pupils to check their answers.
Key 5, 1, 4, 6, 3, 2

Step 2

1 Remind pupils of the song by asking *Who am I?* Mime having a beard that grows in and out. Elicit the name *Michael Finnegan*.

2 Give out worksheet 1 again if necessary. Pupils read the lines of the song in the correct order.

3 Say *Now let's sing the song.* Play the recording. Pupils read the words and sing along.

4 Mime being old and say *Michael Finnegan is old. What's the opposite of old?* (*young*). Then say *His whiskers grew out. What's the opposite of out?* (*in*).

5 Draw pupils' attention to the 'opposites' activity at the bottom of worksheet 1. Explain that Michael Finnegan is fishing for words. Each time they have to find and circle the word in the pool that is the opposite of the one he has 'caught'. Show pupils the example and get them to finish the activity in pairs.
Key 1 old/young, 2 on/under, 3 out/in, 4 begin/stop, 5 catch/throw, 6 fat/thin

6 Check the answers and then sing the song together again.

Step 3

1 Say *Can you remember what Michael Finnegan is doing in the song?* (*fishing*). *Did he catch a fish?* (*Yes*). *What did he do with it?* (*He threw it back into the water!*)

2 Give pupils worksheet 2. Say *You're going to play a game. Help Michael Finnegan go fishing and then go home.* Use the A3 copy of the game to explain how to play. Point to the number 1 and say *Start here.* Show pupils a coin and say *You throw the coin and move. Heads means move ahead one square. Tails means move ahead two squares. The first person to reach Michael Finnegan's home wins.*

3 Point to the squares with instructions on them. Read each instruction with the class and make sure they understand what they have to do if they land on each square.

4 Divide pupils into pairs or small groups and help pupils as necessary as they play the game.

1 Listen and put the sentences in the correct order.

☐ He grew fat and then grew thin again.

1 He had whiskers on his chinnegan.

☐ Caught a fish and threw it in again.

☐ Then he died and had to begin again.

☐ He went fishing with a pinnegan.

☐ They fell out and then grew in again.

2 Find and circle the opposites.

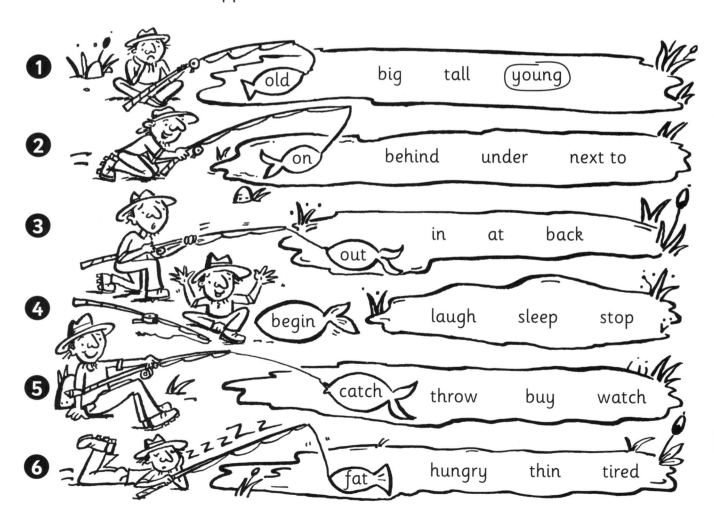

❶ old   big   tall   (young)

❷ on   behind   under   next to

❸ out   in   at   back

❹ begin   laugh   sleep   stop

❺ catch   throw   buy   watch

❻ fat   hungry   thin   tired

Michael Finnegan 2

Play the game. Help Michael Finnegan go fishing and then go home.

Row, row, row your boat

LANGUAGE FOCUS

things by a river
action and 'noise' verbs
*If you see … , don't forget
to …*
the water cycle

LEVEL 2

AGE RANGE 8–10

TIME
Step 1: 15 minutes
Step 2: 20 minutes
Step 3: 15 minutes

MATERIALS

⊙ **124** Lyrics p.137

Step 1
Worksheet 1 for each pupil

Step 2
Worksheet 1 for each pupil
plus 1 x A3 copy

Step 3
Worksheet 2 for each pupil
plus 1 x A3 copy

**FOLLOW-UP
ACTIVITIES**

Class create a similar song
about a car (p.14)

Class do a project on using
and saving water (p.16)

Step 1 Visualising things/animals by a river, listening to the song
Step 2 Learning places you can row to, completing and singing the song
Step 3 Describing the water cycle, drawing yourself using water

---

Step 1

1 Draw simple outlines of different forms of transport, including a rowing boat, on the board. For each one, say *What am I drawing?* and elicit the word.

2 Say *Listen to this. What is it about?* Play verse 1 of the song. Elicit *boat.*

3 Say *Now, row, row, row your boat.* Get pupils to mime rowing. Then pupils continue rowing, but close their eyes. Say *You're rowing down a river. What can you see?* Elicit e.g. *fish, birds, trees, plants, mountains.* Write words on the board.

4 Say *Now you're rowing in Africa. What can you see?* (*elephants, lions,* etc.). Repeat with other countries e.g. Australia (*crocodiles, kangaroos*) or the Arctic (*polar bears, penguins*). Include all the animals in worksheet 1.

5 Give each pupil worksheet 1. Pupils name the things in the pictures by the side of the river and compare with their list on the board. Elicit/Teach any new vocabulary.

6 Say, *What things are in the song? Put a circle round the pictures.* Play the recording.
Key 1 crocodile, 2 polar bear, 3 waterfall, 4 lion, 5 spider

Step 2

1 Say *Where can we row? Look.* Draw on the board pictures of a boat going down a stream / a river / to the shore / in a bath / floating about. Write *to the shore, down the stream, in the bath, down the river, float about* on the board in random order. Get pupils to match them to your pictures. Play the recording. Pupils shout out each expression on the board that they hear. Number them in order from 1 to 5.

2 Teach the words *scream, shiver, shout, roar, laugh.* Get pupils to do the actions quietly!

3 Stick the A3 copy of worksheet 1 on the board and, if necessary, give each pupil a copy. Remind pupils of the things by the river at the top of the worksheet. Pupils fill in the left-hand speech bubbles in the order of the pictures, using the words in the word box.
Key See 6 in Step 1

4 Say e.g. *shiver.* Pupils do the action. Say *If you see a (what?) ……… , don't forget to shiver.* Pupils guess which animal it is (*polar bear*), then, in pairs, try to guess the missing words in the right-hand speech bubbles. Play the recording for them to check and complete the speech bubbles from the word box.
Key 1 scream, 2 shiver, 3 shout, 4 roar, 5 laugh

5 Say *Now let's sing the song.* Play the recording. Pupils sing and roar, shiver, scream, etc. using the speech bubbles to help them.

Step 3

1 Draw some raindrops on the board and say *What's this?* (*rain*). *Where does rain come from?* (*clouds/the sky*). Say *Where does rain go to?* (*rivers and streams*).

2 Say *We're going to learn about rain.* Stick the A3 copy of worksheet 2 on the board. Point to each picture and read aloud the text describing the water cycle. Ask pupils to choose the correct words with you.
Key 1 river, 2 sun, 3 water, 4 clouds, 5 mountains, 6 rain, 7 rivers

3 Give each pupil worksheet 2. Pupils read and circle the correct words.

4 Elicit things that we use water for (*drinking, washing, cooking, swimming, cleaning our teeth*). Pupils draw themselves doing one of these things in the centre of the worksheet.

Row, row, row your boat 1

1   Listen and circle the things in the song.

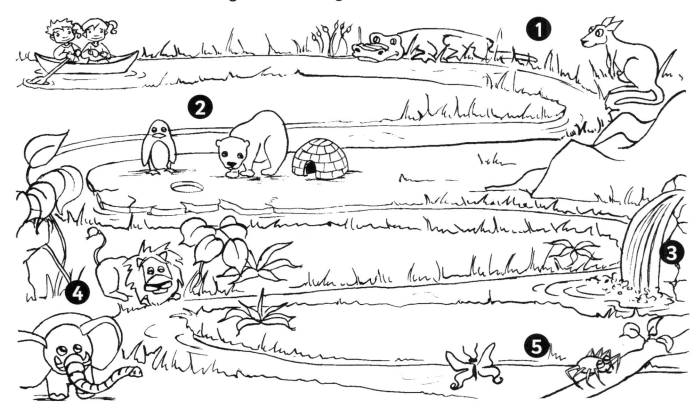

2   Choose, listen and write the words from the song.

| lion   spider   crocodile
waterfall   polar bear | shiver   laugh   shout
scream   roar |

1 (If you see a .... , (don't forget to ....)

2 (If you see a .... , (don't forget to ....)

3 (If you see a .... , (don't forget to ....)

4 (If you see a .... , (don't forget to ....)

5 (If you see a .... , (don't forget to ....)

Circle the correct words in the water cycle. Draw yourself using water.

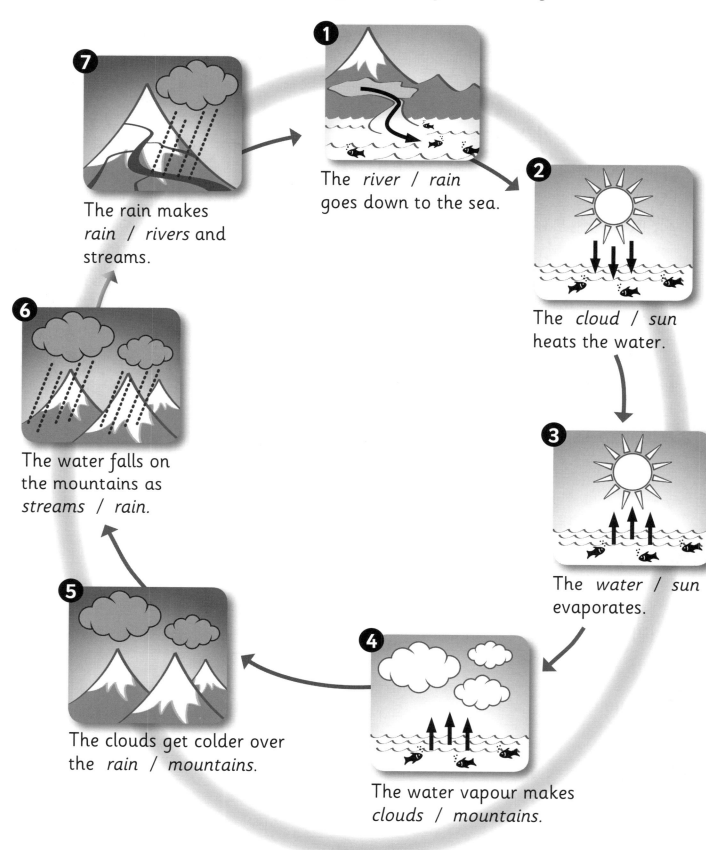

7 The rain makes *rain / rivers* and streams.

1 The *river / rain* goes down to the sea.

2 The *cloud / sun* heats the water.

3 The *water / sun* evaporates.

6 The water falls on the mountains as *streams / rain*.

5 The clouds get colder over the *rain / mountains*.

4 The water vapour makes *clouds / mountains*.

Oranges and lemons

LANGUAGE FOCUS
shopping vocabulary and phrases
When will … ?

LEVEL 2

AGE RANGE 8–10

TIME
Step 1: 20 minutes
Step 2: 20 minutes
Step 3: 30 minutes

MATERIALS
 Lyrics p.137

Step 1
Worksheet 1 for each pupil plus 1 x A3 copy

Step 2
Worksheet 1 for each pupil

Step 3
Worksheet 2 cut into ten individual cards – enough for one card per pupil in each group

FOLLOW-UP ACTIVITIES
Pupils make a shop poster to advertise an ideal shop that sells everything pupils would like to buy (p.16)

Pupils research what their own street or town square looked like in the old days (p.17)

Step 1 Matching the names of the bells and what they say, listening to/chanting the song

Step 2 Acting out a traditional playground 'oranges and lemons' game, naming shops and matching them to products

Step 3 Playing a shopping game

Step 1

1 Give each pupil worksheet 1 and stick the A3 copy on the board. Discuss generally what you can see in the picture.

2 Play the bells ringing on the recording. Say *Where in the picture is this noise coming from?* (*the bells of the church towers*). Read the names of the towers and the speech bubbles and explain meanings as necessary e.g. *farthings* – an old type of British coin. Get pupils to guess what each bell tower is 'saying': they all rhyme (e.g. *Clements* and *lemons*). Play the recording and check, pausing as necessary.
Key c St Clement's, a St Martin's, b Old Bailey, f Shoreditch, d Stepney, e Bow

3 Check by asking pupils to read the conversation in the order of the bell towers.

4 Read aloud the last two lines of the song (p.137). Explain that, in the old days, this might be what happened to a person who took things and didn't pay for them. Get pupils to find someone in the picture who has taken something from a shop without paying!

5 Divide the class into six groups, one for each bell, and do the song as a chant.

Step 2

1 If necessary, give worksheet 1 to each pupil and review what the bells are saying. All pupils say the last two lines.

2 Demonstrate and play the traditional playground game to this song (see p.14).

3 Pupils look at the shops on the worksheet. Say *Where can you buy oranges and lemons?* Teach/Elicit *greengrocer's*. Repeat with *toy shop, baker's, chemist's, clothes shop*.

4 Using the word box, pupils write the names above the shops.

5 Say *What can you buy at the chemist?* Elicit *medicine, soap, plasters*. Repeat with the *baker's – bread, cakes, sandwiches; greengrocer's – apples, oranges, lemons; toy shop – dolls, kites, balls* and the *clothes shop – skirts, T-shirts, trousers*.

Step 3

1 Say *Let's play a shopping game*. Draw some fruit on the board and say *What's my shop?* (*greengrocer's*). Teach/Elicit the shopping dialogue on page 14 and drill.

2 Check vocabulary from the shopping lists in worksheet 2 e.g. *a bottle of medicine, a box of plasters, a bar of soap, a loaf of bread* (plural *loaves*), etc.

3 Copy a shopping list and two 'shop' cards from worksheet 2 onto the board. Act out a couple of purchases with confident pupils to show how a. customers cross things off the shopping list as they buy, b. shopkeepers cross off their cards what they sell.

4 Put pupils into groups of ten. Give each pupil a different card cut out from worksheet 2: five pupils are shopkeepers (they can invent and write a name for their shop and prices, and set up a 'shop', if possible); five pupils are customers with shopping lists. The 'customers' visit each shop in their group in turn until their shopping is complete.

5 Help as necessary. When pupils have finished, ask the shopkeepers what they have left in their shops.
Key greengrocer – one lemon; toyshop – one kite; chemist – one box of plasters; clothes shop – one pair of trousers; baker's – one sandwich

1 Match the bells to what they are saying.

a I owe you five farthings.

b When will you pay me?

c Oranges and lemons.

d When will that be?

e I do not know.

f When I grow rich.

St Clement's   **Old Bailey**   **Bow**

St Martin's   **Shoreditch**   **Stepney**

2 Write the names on the shops.

toy shop   greengrocer's   baker's   chemist's   clothes shop

Oranges and lemons 2

Play the shopping game.

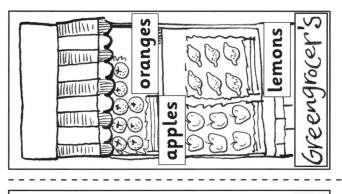

Greengrocer's — oranges, apples, lemons

- Four apples
- Two T-shirts
- A kite
- Two loaves of bread
- One bottle of medicine

Toy Shop — kites, balls, dolls

- Six oranges
- A pair of trousers
- Two dolls
- Three bars of soap
- Two cakes

Chemist's — medicine, soap, plasters

- Two apples
- A skirt
- A doll
- Four sandwiches
- One box of plasters

Clothes Shop — T-shirts, skirts, trousers

- Five lemons
- Three T-shirts
- Two balls
- Three loaves of bread
- Two bars of soap

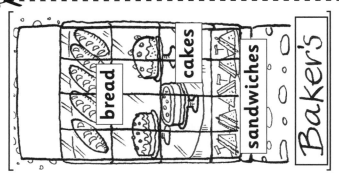

Baker's — bread, cakes, sandwiches

- Two oranges
- Two skirts
- A ball
- A cake
- Two bottles of medicine

3.1 In the Quartermaster's store

LANGUAGE FOCUS
animals and rhyming words
places in the town
giving directions

LEVEL 3

AGE RANGE 10–12

TIME
Step 1: 20 minutes
Step 2: 25 minutes
Step 3: 30 minutes

MATERIALS
⊙ 126 Lyrics p.138

Step 1
Worksheet 1 for each pupil
plus 1 x A3 copy of the
Quartermaster's store picture

Step 2
Worksheet 1 for each pupil
plus 1 x A3 copy

Step 3
Worksheet 2 for each pupil
plus 1 x A3 copy, blank
paper, scissors

FOLLOW-UP ACTIVITIES

Class create a song using
their names e.g. *There was
Sam, eating all the jam* (p.14)

Class make a simple map of
their local area

Step 1 Reviewing/Learning shop items and animals, listening to the song, gap-filling the chorus
Step 2 Working out anagrams, matching rhyming words, singing the song
Step 3 Reading, writing and following directions

Step 1

1 Teach/Elicit a few words for buildings in the local area e.g. *supermarket, bookshop, cinema.* Ask pupils what they buy or do in these places.

2 Stick the A3 picture of the Quartermaster's store from worksheet 1 on the board. Say *What does this shop sell?* Teach/Elicit words including *keys, oats, rakes.* Say *It's a Quartermaster's store* (a supply store for the army). Write the name on the board.

3 Say *There's a problem in the store! What can you see in the picture?* Teach/Elicit the animals' names (*rats, goats, foxes, bears, bees*). Write on the board.

4 Give each pupil worksheet 1. Say *Listen to the song and put a number next to the animals.* Show pupils the number 1 next to the rats. Play the recording. Check.
Key 1 rats, 2 goats, 3 foxes, 4 bears, 5 bees

5 Say *Why are the animals in the shop?* Elicit ideas. Then explain that the Quartermaster can't see them. Focus on his words in the speech bubble. Play the song chorus again, pausing for pupils to write the words.
Key 1 eyes, 2 see, 3 specs

Step 2

1 Get pupils to write as many new words as possible from the words *Quartermaster's store.*

2 If necessary, give each pupil worksheet 1 again and stick the A3 copy on the board. Review the things in the picture. Say *Which animals are hiding/eating/running/buzzing?* (*foxes, goats, bears, bees*)

3 Point out the example anagram in activity 2. Pupils write the animals' names. Check and drill.
Key 1 rats, 2 goats, 3 foxes, 4 bears, 5 bees

4 Explain *alley cats* (big, wild, street cats). Say *Listen. Alley cats. What animals in the picture does that rhyme with?* (*rats*). Show the example in activity 2 (*rats as big as alley cats*). Put pupils into pairs to match the rhymes from the song. Play the recording for pupils to check.
Key 1d, 2a, 3c, 4b, 5e

5 Say *Now let's sing the song.* Then pupils find the Quartermaster's specs hidden in the picture (between the rakes).

Step 3

1 Say *What shops and buildings do we have in our town?* Elicit ideas and list on the board. Give each pupil worksheet 2. Get pupils to check which buildings on the board are on the map already. Add any extra ones to the map.

2 Stick the A3 copy of worksheet 2 on the board. Say *The Quartermaster can't find his specs again. Let's help him find them.* Read and follow the directions on the map with your finger.
Key The specs are in the school.

3 To practise directions, invite individual pupils to the front of the class and give them instructions. (*turn right, turn left, go past my desk,* etc.) Get other pupils to give instructions.

4 Say *Now you're going to practise finding the Quartermaster's specs.* Pupils cut out the specs from the worksheet and decide where on the map they are hidden. They write simple directions (from the Quartermaster's store) to find them. Pupils work in pairs, reading out their directions for their partner to put the glasses in the correct place. Monitor and help.

1 Listen and number the animals. What is the Quartermaster saying?

specs   eyes   see

My .... are dim. I cannot ....
I have not brought my .... with me.

2 Write the animals' names and then match them to what they are doing.

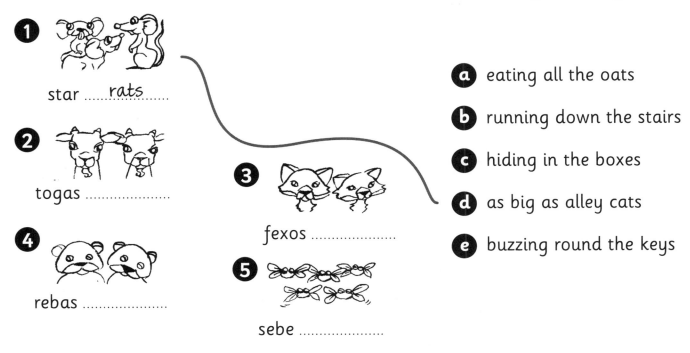

1 star .....rats.....

2 togas ....

3 fexos ....

4 rebas ....

5 sebe ....

a eating all the oats

b running down the stairs

c hiding in the boxes

d as big as alley cats

e buzzing round the keys

Read and find the Quartermaster's specs.

Go out of the store and turn right.
Turn right at the bus stop.
Go past the library on the left and the post office on the right.
Turn left at the bus stop.
Your specs are in the building on the right.
They're in the ...

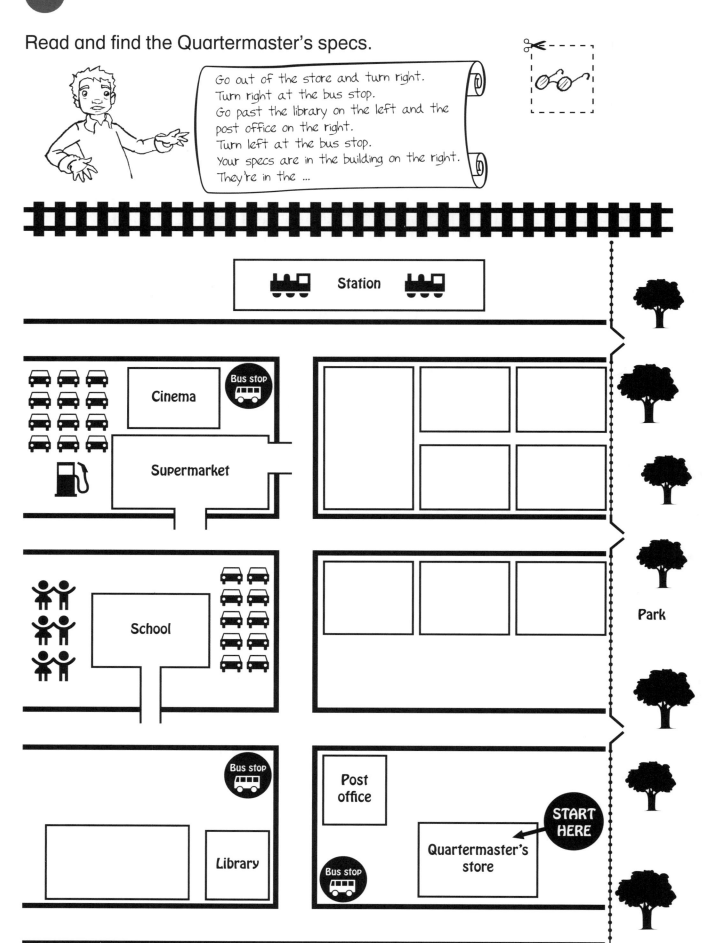

Station

Cinema

Bus stop

Supermarket

School

Post office

Library

Bus stop

Bus stop

START HERE

Quartermaster's store

Park

The house that Jack built

3.2

LANGUAGE FOCUS
animals and people on a farm
people who build houses
action verbs
relative clauses

LEVEL 3

AGE RANGE 10–12

TIME
Step 1: 20 minutes
Step 2: 20 minutes
Step 3: 25 minutes

MATERIALS
🔘127 Lyrics p.138

Step 1
A3 copy of Jack's house from
worksheet 1, worksheet 1 for
each pupil

Step 2
Worksheet 1 for each pupil

Step 3
Worksheet 2 for each pupil
plus 1 x A3 copy

FOLLOW-UP ACTIVITIES
Pupils create their own chant
about the class e.g. *This is the
pupil that threw the book that
hit the teacher on the nose!*

Pupils design their ideal home

Step 1 Reviewing/Learning animals/people on a farm, numbering their order in the chant
Step 2 Completing a gap-fill, chanting
Step 3 Learning about people who build houses

Step 1

1 Stick the A3 copy of the house on the board. Point to the man in the kitchen and say *This is Jack!* Point to the house. Say *This is the house that Jack built.* Write this sentence on the board. Drill.

2 Give each pupil worksheet 1. Using the picture, teach/elicit *dawn, breakfast, cheese, rat, dog* and *cat.* Establish the connection between them e.g. *What's happening to the cheese from Jack's breakfast?* (the rat's eating it), *What's happening to the rat?* (the cat's going to kill it), *What's happening to the cat?* (the dog's chasing it).

3 Read verses 1 and 2 of the chant aloud (see song lyrics p.138). Pupils point to each item in the picture as it's mentioned. Write up the pattern *This is the .... that ....* Get pupils to chant verses 1 and 2 up to *ate the cheese in the house that Jack built.*

4 Say *What else is in the picture?* Elicit/Teach *cow, cockerel, farm girl, farmer, yawn, corn, horn, lawn.* Drill and write on the board.

5 Say *Listen. Point to the people and animals you hear.* Either say verse 3 or play the recording, pointing to the picture on the board. Then play verse 3 again several times. Pupils listen and write numbers next to the characters in worksheet 1. Check.
Key 1 farmer, 2 cockerel, 3 man, 4 farm girl, 5 cow, 6 dog, 7 cat, 8 rat, 9 Jack

Step 2

1 If necessary, give each pupil worksheet 1 again. Elicit the characters in the chant and the 'pattern' sentence.

2 Dot around the board the words *ate, chased, woke, killed, heard, crowed, kissed, scared, built, milked, yawned, sowed.* Check meaning. Give pupils time to look at the picture and think about possible connections. Elicit examples of the 'pattern' in random order e.g. *This is the farm girl that milked the cow* (see song lyrics p.138).

3 Pupils look at the gapped text and word box at the bottom of worksheet 1 and the example. Pupils work in pairs to try to complete the gaps. Play the recording to check.
Key 1 farmer, 2 cockerel, 3 man, 4 farm girl, 5 cow, 6 dog, 7 cat, 8 rat, 9 house, 10 Jack

4 Say *Now let's say it together.* Pupils chant to the recording, using the worksheet to help.

Step 3

1 Say *Jack built a house. Have you seen people building a real house?* Stick the A3 copy of worksheet 2 on the board and give a copy to each pupil. Teach/Elicit aspects of the house including *the plan, bathroom, toilet, kitchen, cupboard, roof, bricks, walls, windows, glass, pipes, lights, wires, washing machine, shelves.*

2 Say *Let's read about people who build houses.* Point out the texts at the top of the picture. Read about the electrician and get the pupils to find her in the picture. Use the A3 copy to show them how to complete her speech bubble with her job title.
Key *I'm the electrician.*

3 Pupils work in pairs, read the texts and complete the speech bubbles for each person. Check and drill the job titles.
Key a electrician, b builder, c architect, d plumber, e carpenter

4 If time, pupils discuss which job they would like to do and why.

93

1 Listen and point. Then number the people and animals.

2 Listen and write the words of the chant.

dog	Jack	cockerel	house	~~farmer~~
man	cat	cow	farm girl	rat

This is the (1) ......farmer...... sowing his corn

That heard the (2) .... crow at dawn

That woke the (3) .... who gave a yawn

That kissed the (4) .... on the lawn

That milked the (5) .... that had one horn

That scared the (6) .... that chased the (7) ....

That killed the (8) .... that ate the cheese

In the (9) .... that (10) .... built.

The house that Jack built 2

Read about the different people who build a house and find them in the picture. Then write the name of each person's job.

1 The electrician is the person who puts in wires for the electricity. It goes to things like the lights, the TV and the washing machine.

2 The carpenter works with wood. He puts in things like doors and cupboards and builds shelves.

3 The architect is the person that designs the house. She draws a plan of the building.

4 The plumber is the person that puts in pipes for the water that goes to the bathroom, toilet and kitchen.

5 The builder is the person that uses the architect's plan to build the house. He builds the walls and roof. He uses bricks, glass and other materials.

On top of spaghetti

LANGUAGE FOCUS
food and drink
rhyming words
restaurant language

LEVEL 3

AGE RANGE 10–12

TIME
Step 1: 20 minutes
Step 2: 25 minutes
Step 3: 25 minutes

MATERIALS

⊙ 128 Lyrics p.139

Step 1
Worksheet 1 for each pupil
plus 1 x A3 picture of the
meatball tree only

Step 2
Worksheet 1 for each pupil,
(approximately 15 flashcard
pictures of single items of
food and drink that pupils
know (numbered), a jumbled
list of the names of the
flashcard items for each pair
of pupils)

Step 3
Worksheet 2 menu cards for
each group plus 1 x A3 copy
of the menu, 'waiter' cards for
each waiter

**FOLLOW-UP
ACTIVITIES**
Pupils categorise food: meat,
cereals, fruit, vegetables,
dairy

Class do a project on food of
their own or another country
(p.16)

Step 1 Listening to the song and tracking the meatball's experiences!
Step 2 Finding rhyming words and completing the song, singing the song, (playing a 'find the food' game)
Step 3 Creating a menu, acting out a restaurant role-play

Step 1

1 Write on the board different countries e.g. *Britain, USA, Italy, China, India* and their foods e.g. *fish and chips, hamburger, pizza, rice, curry* for pupils to match.

2 Say *We're going to listen to a song about food. It's about meatballs, spaghetti, cheese and tomato sauce.* Ask pupils what country they think the song is from (*USA*).

3 Say *Listen. What happened to the meatball in the song?* Play the recording up to *When somebody sneezed.* Elicit where the meatball was and what happened to it.

4 Stick the A3 copy of the meatball tree on the board and give worksheet 1 to each pupil. Say *This is a meatball tree. Can you find the meatballs on top of spaghetti?* Point out the example.

5 Pupils look at the pictures. Say *What happened to one of the meatballs?* Elicit suggestions. Play the recording. Pupils listen and number the meatballs 2 to 10. Check.
Key 1a, 2g, 3b, 4j, 5e, 6f, 7d, 8c, 9h, 10i

Step 2

1 If necessary, remind pupils about the meatball tree. Explain the words at the bottom of worksheet 1 and get pupils to match words in the list that rhyme. (*cheese–sneeze*, etc.)

2 Read the song lines. Explain any vocabulary and complete the first four lines together. Pupils work in pairs to try to complete the song. Say *Now listen again and check.* Play the recording, pausing as necessary.
Key 1 cheese, 2 sneezed, 3 floor, 4 door, 5 bush, 6 mush, 7 be, 8 tree, 9 moss, 10 sauce, 11 cheese, 12 sneeze

3 Say *Let's sing the song.* Play the recording for pupils to sing along.

4 Play a food game. Put the numbered 'food and drink' flashcards round the room and give each pair of pupils a list of the items. The first pair to write each flashcard number next to the correct food word on the list wins.

Step 3

1 Write on the board *What's your favourite food? What country does it come from? Do you go to restaurants sometimes?* Discuss with the class.

2 Say *We're going to play a restaurant game.* Using the A3 menu card from worksheet 2, elicit the restaurant name and explain any new vocabulary.

3 Put pupils into groups of four. Give each group a menu card. Each group agrees on what extra dishes to write in the spaces. Monitor and help with ideas, vocabulary and pronunciation.

4 Present and drill this dialogue:

Waiter	Customer
Hello. Can I help you?	*Yes. Can I have fish and chips, please?*
Yes, of course. What would you like to drink?	*Orange juice, please.*
Would you like anything else?	*No, thank you.*

5 Pupils work in their groups of four: one waiter and three customers. Give each waiter the 'waiter card' from worksheet 2 to take the order. Groups act out the dialogue.

6 Monitor and help. Pupils swap roles, then act out their dialogues for the class.

On top of spaghetti 1

1 Listen to the song and number the meatballs.

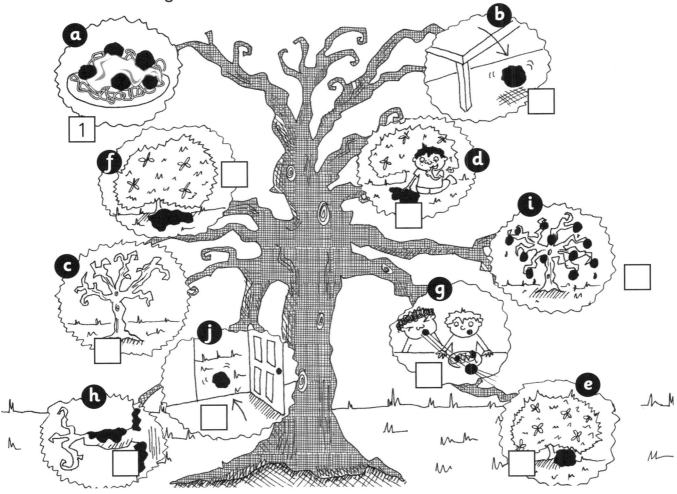

2 Listen and write the rhyming words in the song.

On top of spaghetti, all covered with ....cheese.............. ,

I lost my poor meatball, when somebody ....

It rolled off the table, and onto the .... ,

And then my poor meatball, rolled out of the ....

It rolled in the garden, and under a .... ,

And then my poor meatball, was nothing but ....

The mush was as tasty, as tasty could .... ,

And then the next summer, grew into a ....

The tree was all covered, all covered with .... ,

And on it grew meatballs, and tomato .... ,

So if you eat spaghetti, all covered with .... ,

Hold onto your meatball, if you start to ....

sauce
be
door
~~cheese~~
bush
sneezed
floor
moss
sneeze
tree
cheese
mush

Complete the menu. Then play a restaurant game.

≈≈≈ BLUE MOON ≈≈≈
Restaurant

Starters

Mixed salad of tomato, cucumber and lettuce

Onion soup and bread

....

....

Main courses

Fish and chips with peas

Roast chicken with potatoes and carrots

....

....

Desserts

Fruit salad of pear, banana, strawberries and melon

Bananas, ice cream and chocolate sauce

....

....

Drinks

Mineral water

Orange juice

....

....

≈≈≈ BLUE MOON ≈≈≈
Restaurant

Waiter name _____

Table number _____

Number of customers _____

Starters	Desserts
Main courses	Drinks

Land of the silver birch

LANGUAGE FOCUS
Canadian nature and animals

LEVEL 3

AGE RANGE 10–12

TIME
Step 1: 20 minutes
Step 2: 20 minutes
Step 3: 25 minutes

MATERIALS
◎ 129 Lyrics p.139

Step 1
Map of the world or globe, pictures and information about Canada, worksheet 1 for each pupil plus 1 x A3 copy

Step 2
Worksheet 1 for each pupil, (colouring pencils)

Step 3
Worksheet 2 for each pupil plus 1 x A3 copy, scissors, blank A4 paper, colouring pencils

FOLLOW-UP ACTIVITIES
Pupils research and design a poster for an area of natural beauty (p.16)

Pupils make totem poles for animals from their country

Step 1 Introducing Canada and native Canadians, listening to the song, learning a drum beat

Step 2 Completing the words of the song, singing the song, (colouring the picture)

Step 3 Reading about animal totems and making a personalised totem pole

---

Step 1

1 Get pupils to point to Canada on the map/globe. Say *What do you know about Canada?* Use pictures to help as necessary.

2 Give each pupil worksheet 1 and stick the A3 copy on the board. Point to the man on the lake. Say *This is a native Canadian. What is he travelling in?* (*a canoe*). Ask where he sleeps and teach/elicit *wigwam*.

3 Use the small pictures to teach *lake, hills, beaver, moose, silver birch, shore, ledge*. Get pupils to match them to the main picture. Pupils then describe the picture e.g. *The moose is next to the lake / standing on the shore*, etc.

4 Say *This is the man's home in the north. He's not there today and he's missing it, so he's singing a song about it. Now listen to the song and point to what you hear in the picture.* Play the recording.

5 Replay the last line of the chorus (*Boom-diddy-ah-da*). Explain/Elicit that this is the drums from the man's village in the north, calling him home. Get pupils to say these words and to drum the rhythm with their hands on the desks.

Step 2

1 If necessary, give each pupil worksheet 1 again. Use it to play a game of I-spy. Say e.g. *I spy with my little eye, something beginning with 'b'.* Pupils guess the item in the picture (*beaver*).

2 Point out the song text, explaining vocabulary as necessary. Explain that the gaps in the song are the words next to the small pictures. Pupils work in pairs and discuss which words go in the gaps. Then say *Now listen to the song and write the letter for the pictures in the gaps.* Play the recording, pausing as necessary. Check.
Key b, g, a, h, d, f, c, e

3 Say *Let's sing the song.* Play the recording for pupils to sing and drum.

4 If time, sing the song as a round (p.13) or get pupils to colour the picture.

Step 3

1 Remind pupils that the song is from Canada. Give each pupil worksheet 2 and stick the A3 copy on the board. Point to the totem pole and say *Do you know what this is?* Explain that totem poles tell stories about animals and families. The animals in this totem pole all come from Canada. Elicit/Teach *bear, owl, beaver, falcon*.

2 Say *People in Canada think that animals are like people. Which animals do you think are friendly?* (*bear, owl*). Read through the sentences about the animals, explaining vocabulary as necessary.

3 Put pupils into pairs or small groups. Say *Which animal are you?* Pupils read the descriptions again and decide which animal they are most like. They then feed back to the class.

4 Pupils cut out and colour animal totems for their group, based on what animals they think they are. They then stick them onto a piece of paper to make a totem pole for their group. Completed totem poles can be displayed in the class.

1 Find the things in the picture. Then listen and point.

a moose

b silver birch

c wigwam

d shore

e hills

f ledge

g beaver

h lake

2 Listen and write the letters in the words of the song.

Land of the [b]
Home of the [ ]
Where still the mighty [ ]
Wanders at will.

Blue [ ] and rocky [ ]
I will return once more.
Boom-diddy-ah-da, boom-diddy-ah-da,
Boom-diddy-ah-da, boom.

High on a rocky [ ]
I'll build my [ ]
Close to the water's edge,
Silent and still.

My heart grows sick for you,
Here in the lowlands.
I will return to you
[ ] of the north.

Land of the silver birch 2

1   Read about the animal totems. Which animal are you?

Beavers are leaders. They like to do jobs quickly. They are very clever. They can be kind and helpful.

Bears are good at doing things with their hands. They are friendly. They can be generous. Sometimes they are shy. They make good teachers.

Owls love adventure. They are very friendly. They are good at lots of things. They can be careless sometimes. Owls make good artists.

Snakes make good doctors. They are helpful and caring but sometimes they are cross. They are funny.

Deer are funny and clever. They like talking and they love parties. But they can also be lazy.

Falcons are leaders. They are very clever and they always have lots of ideas. They like looking at themselves.

2   Make a totem pole for your group.

3.5

London Bridge is falling down

LANGUAGE FOCUS
natural materials
big numbers
years and decimal numbers
superlatives
question word questions

LEVEL 3

AGE RANGE 10–12

TIME
Step 1: 25 minutes
Step 2: 15 minutes
Step 3: 35 minutes

MATERIALS
 Lyrics p.140

Step 1
Objects made from different materials, worksheet 1 for each pupil

Step 2
Worksheet 1 for each pupil

Step 3
Worksheet 2 cut up into one fact card per pupil

FOLLOW-UP ACTIVITIES
Class do a poster project on what different objects are made of (p.16)

Class research famous bridges or monuments in their country (p.17)

Step 1 Learning materials vocabulary, listening to the song, talking about bridges
Step 2 Matching 'bridge' sentences from the song, singing the song, (thinking about materials)
Step 3 Saying years and numbers, asking for and giving facts about famous bridges

Step 1

1 Say *What's my pencil made of?* Elicit *wood*. Use other objects to teach the materials listed in the key in 2 below. Pass the objects round. Pupils say the material as they touch them.

2 Give each pupil worksheet 1. Get them to use the word box to label the pictures. Check.
Key 1 wood, 2 silver, 3 plastic, 4 iron, 5 steel, 6 paper, 7 clay, 8 gold, 9 stone, 10 wool

3 Draw a simple bridge on the board. Say *This is a famous bridge. We're going to listen to a song about it. What's its name and what's the problem with it?* Play verse 1 of the song. Elicit (*London Bridge*) and (*It's falling down*).

4 Say *What can we use to mend London Bridge? Listen to the song and tick the materials you hear.* Play the whole recording. Check.
Key wood, clay, iron, steel, silver, gold, stone
Ask pupils what the builders used, then listen again (*stone*).

5 Pupils name bridges they know. For each ask *Where is it? What is it made of?* Discuss.

Step 2

1 If necessary, elicit the problem with London Bridge and give each pupil worksheet 1.

2 Elicit that the new bridge will be of *stone*. Elicit the other materials. Say *London Bridge goes over water. Why is clay not a very good material?* (*the water can wash it away*). Pupils look at the broken bridges and match 1 and b. Say *Listen to the song and make the other bridges.* Play the recording. **Key** 1b, 2d, 3c, 4a

3 Check answers and do the actions: *wash away* (move your hands away from you as if they are floating away), *bend and bow* (bend an iron bar), *will be stolen away* (mime running away with something, *last so long* (fold arms in front of you as if very firm and tight).

4 Say *Let's sing the song.* Play the recording. Pupils sing and do the actions in two groups.

5 If time, pupils can discuss what things around them are made of and why e.g. *Notebooks are made of paper because you can write on paper.*

Step 3

1 Write some 'big numbers' e.g. *4,912; 2,862* on the board. Teach/Elicit how to say them. Repeat for years e.g. *1673* and decimal numbers e.g. *12.3.* Dictate some numbers for pupils to write down. Check. (If time, pupils work in pairs and dictate numbers to their partner.)

2 Say *We're going to think about some famous bridges. What questions can you ask about a bridge?* Elicit and write on the board *Where is it?; When was it finished?; How long is it?; What is it made of? How much did it cost?* Drill.

3 Put pupils into groups of four. Give each pupil in the group a different fact card. They must not look at each other's cards. Write the names of the four bridges on the board.

4 Pupils complete their fact cards by asking and answering the questions in their groups. Regroup pupils into 'bridge' groups, to check facts for their bridge.

5 Write on the board, in full, the following seven questions *Which is the 1 longest / 2 shortest / 3 newest / 4 most expensive / 5 oldest bridge? 6 Which bridge is in San Francisco? 7 Which bridges are made of steel?* Check meaning. Give pupils time to find the answers.
Key 1, 3, 4 – Akashi Kaikyo Bridge; 2 Tower Bridge; 5 Firth of Forth Bridge; 6 Golden Gate Bridge; 7 All of them

6 Finish by asking *Which is the best bridge?* and taking a class vote.

1   Write the materials. Then tick (✓) the ones you hear in the song.

wool	steel	paper	stone	~~wood~~
silver	plastic	clay	gold	iron

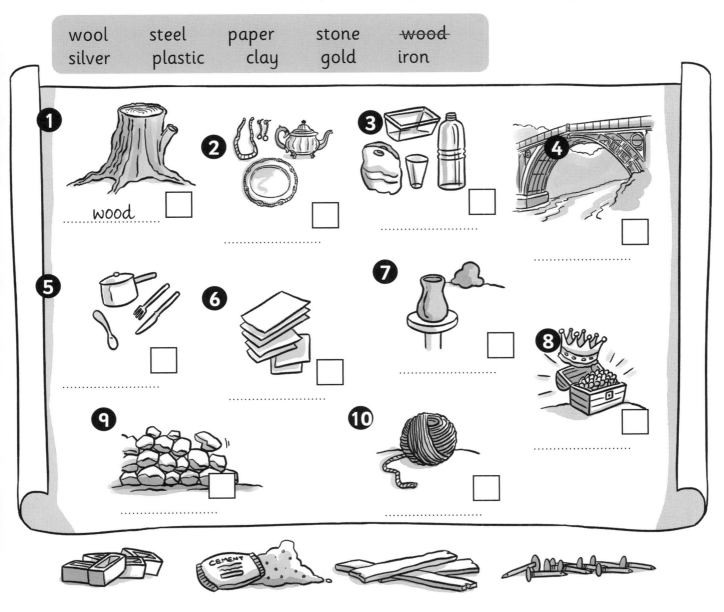

1   wood   ☐

2   .... ☐

3   .... ☐

4   .... ☐

5   .... ☐

6   .... ☐

7   .... ☐

8   .... ☐

9   .... ☐

10   .... ☐

2   Listen, read and make the bridges.

1 Wood and clay

2 Iron and steel

3 Silver and gold

4 Stone so strong

a will last so long.

b will wash away.

c will be stolen away.

d will bend and bow.

Talk to your friends and complete the information about these famous bridges.

Name of bridge	Location	Finished	Length	Materials used	Cost
Tower Bridge	London, England	1894	268 metres	steel, stone	£1 million
Firth of Forth Bridge					
Akashi Kaikyo Bridge					
Golden Gate Bridge					

Name of bridge	Location	Finished	Length	Materials used	Cost
Tower Bridge					
Firth of Forth Bridge	Queensferry, Scotland	1890	2,523 metres	steel	$15 million
Akashi Kaikyo Bridge					
Golden Gate Bridge					

Name of bridge	Location	Finished	Length	Materials used	Cost
Tower Bridge					
Firth of Forth Bridge					
Akashi Kaikyo Bridge	Kobe Japan	1998	3,910 metres	steel	$4.3 billion
Golden Gate Bridge					

Name of bridge	Location	Finished	Length	Materials used	Cost
Tower Bridge					
Firth of Forth Bridge					
Akashi Kaikyo Bridge					
Golden Gate Bridge	San Francisco	1937	2,737 metres	steel, concrete	$27 million

The green grass grew all around

3.6

LANGUAGE FOCUS
trees and nature
'environment' vocabulary

LEVEL 3

AGE RANGE 10–12

TIME
Step 1: 20 minutes
Step 2: 20 minutes
Step 3: 20 minutes

MATERIALS
⊙ 131 Lyrics p.140

Step 1
Worksheet 1 for each pupil

Step 2
Worksheet 1 for each pupil

Step 3
Worksheet 2 for each pupil,
(poster paper, scissors, glue,
colouring pencils)

**FOLLOW-UP
ACTIVITIES**
Pupils do a project on things
that come from trees (p.16)

Pupils make a questionnaire
to ask people how they help
the environment (p.17)

Step 1 Reviewing/Learning vocabulary for the song, labelling a picture, listening to the song
Step 2 Choosing words for the song, learning actions, singing the song
Step 3 Looking at what trees do for our environment, considering ways of looking after trees

Step 1

1 Draw a simple diagram of a hole in the ground with grass growing round it. Elicit *grass, ground* and *hole*. Say *I'm going to draw something in the hole. What is it?* Pupils guess and when they say *a tree*, draw the tree in the hole. Continue eliciting and drawing in the following order: *branch, leaves, nest, bird, wings, feathers*.

2 Give each pupil worksheet 1. Say *Look at the words in the wordbox and label the picture*. Monitor and check.

3 Say *Now listen to this song. Tick the words you hear*. Play the recording. Ask pupils which words they ticked.
Key all the words should be ticked except *leaves* and *wings*

4 To help with memorising vocabulary, get pupils to secretly choose a word from the worksheet and do an action for the others to shout out the word.

Step 2

1 If necessary, remind pupils of the song and give each pupil worksheet 1 again. Focus on the lines from the song. Pupils work in pairs to choose the best word for each line. Play the recording for them to circle the correct word, pausing as necessary.
Key tree, branch, nest, bird, feathers

2 Demonstrate the following actions to perform while pupils are singing the song.
In that hole (make a circle with your arms)
There was a tree (stand up and stretch your arms over your head)
There was a branch (reach one of your arms out to the side)
There was a nest (cup your hand and hold facing upwards)
There was a bird (move your fingers and thumb like a beak snapping together)
There were some feathers (stroke your arm as though preening your feathers)

3 Say *Let's sing the song together*. Pupils sing along, using the worksheet to help them.

Step 3

1 Say *Where can you see trees?* Elicit possible answers (*gardens, parks, forests*). Say *Why do we need trees?* Accept any suggestions, then say *Trees are very important. Let's find out why.*

2 Give each pupil worksheet 2. Focus on the pictures to see whether any of the ideas have already been mentioned. Then read and check the meaning of the sentences. Say *Now read and write the letters next to the pictures*. Check.
Key 1d, 2b, 3e, 4f, 5c, 6a

3 In pairs pupils read the sentences again and rank them in importance. Discuss.

4 Say *Trees are important. So how can we look after them?* Look at the two ideas on worksheet 2. Get pupils to write their own idea in the empty speech bubble, then feed back as a class e.g. *plant more trees, stop cutting down trees, recycle paper, don't waste paper, set up nature reserves.*

5 If time, cut out pupils' ideas and put them on a decorated classroom 'Save the Trees' poster.

1 Label the picture. Then listen to the song and tick (✓) the words you hear.

| branch | bird | leaves | ~~tree~~ | nest | hole |
| feathers | grass | wing | ground | | |

tree

2 Read the lines from the song. Then listen and circle the correct word.

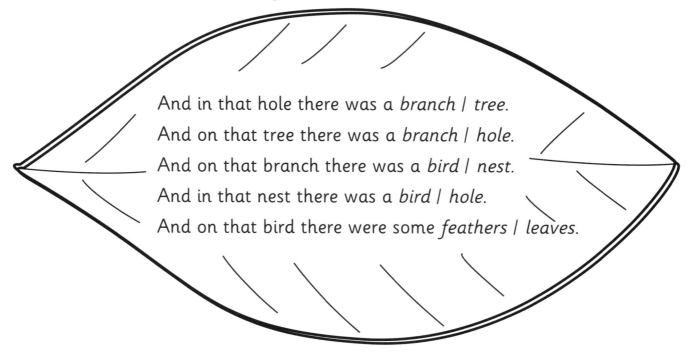

And in that hole there was a *branch* / *tree*.
And on that tree there was a *branch* / *hole*.
And on that branch there was a *bird* / *nest*.
And in that nest there was a *bird* / *hole*.
And on that bird there were some *feathers* / *leaves*.

The green grass grew all around 2

1 Why do we need trees? Read and match.

a Trees give us wood. We need wood to build houses and make furniture.

b Trees give us oxygen. We need oxygen to breathe.

c Tree roots hold the soil and stop it going into the rivers.

d Trees give a home to many animals and insects.

e Some of our food and medicine comes from trees.

f Trees give us shade from the sun. They also give shelter from wind and rain.

2 Trees are important. How can we look after them? Write your idea.

Keep the air clean!

Don't make furniture from very old trees!

....
....

3.7

As I was going to St Ives

LANGUAGE FOCUS
riddles and puzzles

LEVEL 3

AGE RANGE 10–12

TIME
Step 1: 15 minutes
Step 2: 20 minutes
Step 3: 15 minutes

MATERIALS
🔘 **132** lyrics p.141

Step 1
Worksheet 1 for each pupil

Step 2
Worksheet 1 for each pupil

Step 3
Worksheet 2 for each pupil
plus 1 x A3 copy

FOLLOW-UP ACTIVITIES
Pupils think of a joke or riddle to tell the class

Play a game of Twenty questions to guess zoo animals (p.16)

Step 1 Introducing the idea of riddles, ordering the rhyme and working out the riddle
Step 2 Gap-filling the words, saying the rhyme, solving more riddles
Step 3 Solving a logic puzzle

Step 1

1 Write on the board and say *Mr and Mrs Muddle have six daughters. Each daughter has one brother. How many people are there in the Muddle family?* Elicit possible answers but don't confirm.

2 Get pupils to draw the Muddle family on the board. There should be nine people: the mother and father, six girls and one boy, who is a brother to all the girls! Explain that this is called a 'riddle'.

3 Say *Now let's listen to another riddle. What number can you hear a lot?* Play the recording.
Key seven

4 Give each pupil worksheet 1. Pupils look at the pictures. Say *Now listen again and number the pictures.* Play the recording then check.
Key 1c, 2f, 3b, 4a, 5e, 6d

5 Say *How many people and things are in the story?* Draw a pyramid diagram on the board (1 storyteller + 1 man + 7 wives + 49 sacks + 343 cats + 2401 kittens = 2802).

6 Say *In the last line, it asks how many were going to St Ives? What's the answer?* The answer is *one*. Read the first line *As I was going to St Ives, I met a man with seven wives.* All the other people were coming from St Ives!

Step 2

1 If necessary, give each pupil worksheet 1 again. Get pupils to look at the words in the word box and write them under the pictures. Check.
Key a cats, b sacks, e kittens, f wives

2 Say *Now let's say the rhyme together.* Play the recording for pupils to follow.

3 Point to the riddles at the bottom of the worksheet and read each one aloud. Help with vocabulary as necessary. Then put pupils into pairs to try to work the riddles out. After a few minutes write the answers, unnumbered, on the board in a jumbled order.
Key 1 all animals – houses can't jump!, 2 your name, 3 a hole, 4 a window
Pupils decide which is the answer to each riddle. Check with the whole class.

Step 3

1 Say *Let's do a logic puzzle!* Give each pupil worksheet 2 and read out the introduction. Check comprehension by asking e.g. *Where are the children? What are they going to see? How many girls are there? What are they eating?* etc.

2 Using the A3 copy of the worksheet look at the pictures. Say *What are the boys'/girls' names? What snacks are they eating? What animals do they like?* Elicit words and drill.

3 Look at the table and read clues 1 and 2. Say *We know that William is the oldest and that he is first in the queue. What else do we know about William? Look at clue number 2.* (*He likes candyfloss.*) Write *William* and *candyfloss* in the 'Snack' column on your A3 worksheet for pupils to copy. Give pupils time to read the other clues. Then ask them what they know e.g. *Who's fourth in the queue (at the back)?* (*Sarah*), *Who likes ice cream?* (*Tony*). *What are Kim's favourite animals?* etc.

4 Put pupils into pairs. Give them time to work out the puzzle. Monitor and help. Check.
Key 1st William — hippos, candyfloss; 2nd Kim – tigers, crisps; 3rd Tony – monkeys, ice cream; 4th Sarah – giraffes, popcorn

1   Listen and number the pictures. Then write the words.

a Every sack had seven
....

b Every wife had seven
....

c As I was going to St Ives

d Kittens, cats, sacks and wives,
How many were going to St Ives?

e Every cat had seven
....

f I met a man with seven
....

kittens   sacks   wives   cats

2   Try these riddles.

1 What animal can jump higher than a house?

2 This belongs to you, but other people use it more than you. What is it?

3 I weigh nothing, but you can see me. Put me in a bucket and I'll make it lighter. What am I?

4 In many parts of the world, there is something which helps you see through walls. What is it?

Read the clues and solve this puzzle. Use the table to help you.

Four children are visiting the zoo. There are two girls and two boys. Two of the children are twins. Each child is excited about seeing their favourite animal. They are waiting in the queue outside the zoo and eating their favourite snacks.

Clues

1. All of the other children are younger than William, but Kim is the youngest.

2. The oldest child, who is eating candyfloss, is first in the queue.

3. Tony drops his ice cream.

4. The twins are the last two in the queue. The twin who is eating ice cream loves the monkeys.

5. Sarah, at the back, loves popcorn.

6. Kim is enjoying her crisps, and is very excited about seeing the tigers.

7. The child who wants to see the giraffes also likes popcorn.

8. The child who likes candyfloss wants to see the hippos.

Order in queue	Child's name	Favourite animal	Snack
1st			
2nd			
3rd			
4th			

The twelve days of Christmas

3.8

LANGUAGE FOCUS
ordinal numbers,
dates 'presents' in the song
truffle recipe ingredients and
cooking instructions

LEVEL 3

AGE RANGE 10–12

TIME
Step 1: 30 minutes
Step 2: 20 minutes
Step 3: 25 minutes

MATERIALS
◎133 Lyrics p.141

Step 1
Flashcards of the pictures in
worksheet 1, set of cut-up
pictures from worksheet 1 for
each pair of pupils

Step 2
Set of cut-up picture cards and
word cards from worksheet 1
for each pair of pupils, (card,
glue, colouring pencils)

Step 3
Worksheet 2 for each pupil,
(some truffles made from
the recipe, examples of
ingredients and equipment),
scissors, glue, (ribbon)

**FOLLOW-UP
ACTIVITIES**
Pupils find out about other
important dates round the
world e.g. *4th July* (American
Independence Day), *14th July*
(French national day) (p.17)

Pupils make the Christmas
truffles in class (p.17)

Step 1 Learning/Reviewing ordinal numbers, listening to the song and putting pictures in order

Step 2 Matching pictures and song words, singing the song

Step 3 Making a Christmas truffles recipe

Step 1

1 Teach/Review ordinal numbers by getting 12 pupils to stand in a line. Drill *first, second*, etc. then call out random ordinal numbers. Pupils say the name of that person in the line.

2 Write *25th December* on the board and say *What day is this?* (Christmas Day). Do the same with *24th December* (Christmas Eve), *26th December* (Boxing Day), *31st December* (New Year's Eve) and *1st January* (New Year's Day).

3 Say *Let's listen to a song about Christmas. How many days can you hear?* Play the last verse of the recording and elicit *12 days* (the days from Christmas Day to 5th January).

4 Say *In the song, every day the singer gets presents from somebody who loves him or her. Did you hear any of them?* Elicit ideas. Then use the flashcards out of order to present them e.g. *a partridge in a pear tree, three turtle doves.* Demonstrate actions e.g. *lords a-leaping.*

5 Give each pair of pupils a set of cut-up picture cards. Say *Listen again and order the pictures.* Play the whole recording, pausing as necessary.

6 Check by writing on the board *On the first day of Christmas my true love sent to me … .* List the ordinal numbers underneath each other. Invite pupils to stick the correct picture on the board.

Step 2

1 Put pupils into pairs. If necessary, give each pair the jumbled cut-up picture cards. Say *Put the cards in order.* Check and point out that the number of presents matches the day of Christmas e.g. *3rd day – three French hens.*

2 Give the sets of word cards to each pair of pupils. Get them to match each card with the appropriate picture. Say *Now listen and check.* Play the last verse of the recording. Monitor and drill.

3 Say *Now let's sing the song together.* Play the recording. Pupils sing along.

4 If you have time, pupils can choose some of the picture cards to make a Christmas card for their family.

Step 3

1 If necessary, remind pupils of the Christmas presents in the song. Then say *We're going to look at a Christmas present you can make for your family.* If you have made some truffles, show them to the class or show examples of the ingredients.

2 Give each pupil worksheet 2. Say *This is a recipe for the truffles.* Teach the names of the ingredients in picture 1 (*cocoa powder, icing sugar, chopped nuts, cream cheese, chocolate strands*) and explain the measurements in the recipe (*50g* and *25g*) if necessary.

3 Teach/Elicit *mixing bowl* and *wooden spoon* and the verbs *put (something) into, stir* and *roll* from the pictures.

4 Read the jumbled recipe instructions aloud, then put pupils into pairs to match the instructions to the correct pictures. Check.
   Key 1c, 2e, 3b, 4d, 5f, 6a

5 Give out scissors and glue. Say *Now make the recipe card.* Pupils cut out the recipe instructions and stick each one next to the correct picture. They can then colour the recipe card, tie it with ribbon or wrap it up to take home.

111

1 Listen and put the pictures in the correct order.

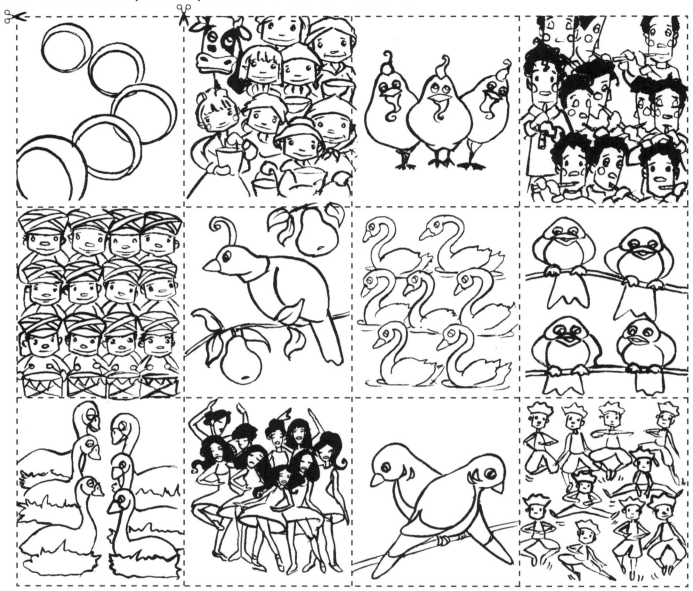

2 Listen and match the words and pictures.

four calling birds	a partridge in a pear tree	three French hens	two turtle doves
seven swans a-swimming	eight maids a-milking	five gold rings	six geese a-laying
ten lords a-leaping	nine ladies dancing	twelve drummers drumming	eleven pipers piping

The twelve days of Christmas 2

Make a Christmas truffles recipe.

Christmas truffles

1
- 25g cocoa powder
- ICING SUGAR
- COCOA POWDER
- CREAM CHEESE
- CHOCOLATE STRANDS
- 50g icing sugar
- 50g cream cheese
- 50g chopped nuts
- chocolate strands

2

3

4

5

6

a Put the truffles into sweet cases.

b Stir the mixture together with a wooden spoon.

c Get cocoa powder, icing sugar, chopped nuts, cream cheese and chocolate strands.

d Roll the mixture into small balls.

e Put the cheese, nuts, icing sugar and cocoa into a mixing bowl.

f Roll each truffle in the chocolate strands.

2 Take the recipe card home and make truffles for your family!

HAPPY XMAS

Happy Christmas

3.9

When I first came to this land

LANGUAGE FOCUS
rhyming words
family and farm vocabulary

LEVEL 3

AGE RANGE 10–12

TIME
Step 1: 20 minutes
Step 2: 25 minutes
Step 3: 20 minutes

MATERIALS
🎵 **134** Lyrics p.142

Step 1
Flashcard of man from
worksheet 1, worksheet 1 for
each pupil

Step 2
Worksheet 1 for each pupil
plus 1 x A3 copy

Step 3
Flashcards of pictures in
worksheet 2, worksheet 2
for each pupil cut up into 8
picture cards, 4 instruction
cards and a playing board

**FOLLOW-UP
ACTIVITIES**
Pupils make a poster of the
pioneer's homestead (p.16)

Pupils find out about farms in
their own country (p.17)

Step 1 Thinking about what pioneers need to start a new life, listening to the song
Step 2 Finding the rhyming words and singing the song
Step 3 Playing a 'Pioneer' game

Step 1

1 Show pupils the flashcard of the man. Say *This young man has nothing. He's going to start a new life in America.* Explain *pioneer.* Elicit what he will need e.g *money, land, a house,* etc. and write on the board.

2 Give each pupil worksheet 1. Read through the jumbled sentences of verse 1. Explain meaning as necessary. Say *Listen and number the lines.* Play verse 1. Check.
   Key 1c, 2a, 3d, 4b

3 Say *Is the pioneer's new life going to be easy?* Point out clues from verse 1: (*no money in his hands, building the shack will break his back*), but he can grow food on the land.

4 Say *The pioneer wants to start a farm. What does he need?* Elicit *buildings, tools* and *animals* and write on the board. Include *cow* and *horse.*

5 Say *Does he want to live alone on the farm?* (No). *What else does he need?* (a family). Add family words to the board. Include *wife, daughter* and *son.*

6 Say *Listen to the man singing about his life. Which words can you hear?* Play the recording. Pupils put up their hands when they hear a word.

Step 2

1 If necessary, give each pupil worksheet 1 again and ask questions about the song e.g. *Where did the pioneer go?* (to America). *Did he have any money? What did he do?*

2 Stick the A3 copy of worksheet 1 on the board. Point to the pictures on the inner circle of the waterwheel. Pupils read the labels.

3 Point to picture 1 on the outer waterwheel circle. Say *When I first came to this **land**. I had no money in my **hand**,* emphasising the rhyme.

4 Point to picture 2 and elicit *shack.* Elicit *back* from the word box to rhyme with *shack.* Put pupils in pairs to choose and write the rhyming words.

5 Play the recording, pausing for pupils to check, then check in whole class.
   Key 1 hand, 2 back, 3 arm, 4 course, 5 now, 6 life, 7 water, 8 done

6 Discuss whether the pioneer had a hard or easy life in the end.

7 Say *Now let's sing the song.* Pupils sing the song, using the waterwheel to help.

Step 3

1 Say *Now we are pioneers! We want to make a farm. What do we need?* Elicit ideas. Use flashcards to explain words for the game *farmhouse, animal shelter, fences, tools, seeds.*

2 Give each pupil a set of cut-up picture and instruction cards and a playing board from worksheet 2. Put the class into small groups. Give each group an extra set of pictures.

3 Groups shuffle all the picture cards together, deal out eight cards each, then mix the rest with the instuction cards in a pile, face down, in the centre.

4 • The idea of the game is for pupils to cover the spaces on the playing board with appropriate pictures. The first to collect a complete farm is the winner.
   • In turn, pupils take a card from the top of the pile.
   • If the card is something they need for their farm, they put it on their board and put one of their other cards at the bottom of the central pile. If they don't need it, they replace it on top.
   • If they take an instruction card, they must follow the instructions before replacing it.
   • The first person to fill the board with pictures shouts out *I'm a pioneer!*

When I first came to this land 1

1 Listen and number the sentences.

a So I got myself a shack. I did what I could. ☐

b But the land was sweet and good. I did what I could. ☐

c When I first came to this land, I had no money in my hand. ☐

d And I called my shack *Break my back.* ☐

2 Look at the waterwheel and complete the words of the song.

done	arm	now	course	water	back	~~hand~~	life

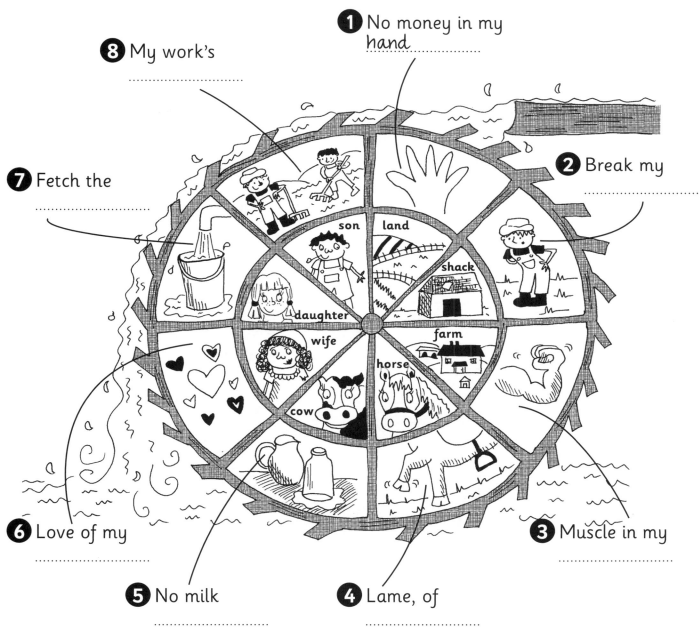

8 My work's ....

1 No money in my hand ....

7 Fetch the ....

2 Break my ....

6 Love of my ....

3 Muscle in my ....

5 No milk ....

4 Lame, of ....

son   land   shack   daughter   wife   farm   horse   cow

Play the pioneer game.

farmhouse	animal shelter	land	fences
family	tools	animals	seeds
Swap a card with the player on your left.	Swap a card with the player on your left.	Swap a card with the player on your right.	Swap a card with the player on your right.

| farmhouse | animal shelter | land | fences |
| family | tools | animals | seeds |

There's a hole in my bucket

LANGUAGE FOCUS

things needed to mend a bucket
to for purpose
too + adjective
things to take on a camping trip

LEVEL 3

AGE RANGE 10–12

TIME

Step 1: 25 minutes
Step 2: 20 minutes
Step 3: 20 minutes

MATERIALS

💿 135 Lyrics p.142

Step 1
Worksheet 1 for each pupil plus 1 x A3 copy

Step 2
Worksheet 1 for each pupil plus 1 x A3 copy

Step 3
Worksheet 2 for each group of three or four pupils plus 1 x A3 copy

FOLLOW-UP ACTIVITIES

Teams of pupils compete to write down as many uses as possible for ten everyday objects

Pupils play Snap with cards from worksheet 2 (p.15)

Step 1 Labelling items in the song, listening to the song and understanding the joke
Step 2 Matching problems and solutions from the song, singing the song
Step 3 Planning what to take on a camping trip

Step 1

1 Say *I'm thirsty. Where can I get some water?* Teach/Elicit *from a tap.*

2 Stick the A3 copy of worksheet 1 on the board. Introduce *Henry* and *Liza*. Say *Did they have a tap in their house, do you think?* Explain/Elicit that, a long time ago, people had to get water from a *well* with a *bucket*. Using the picture, teach/elicit *bucket, hole, water, knife, straw, well* and *stone.*

3 Give each pupil worksheet 1. Pupils look at the example and use the words in the word box to label the picture. Check.

4 Ask questions to get pupils to think about the relationship between the things in the picture e.g. *What's the problem with Henry's bucket?* (*there's a hole in it*); *What do you need a bucket for?* (*to get water*), etc. Write *You need a bucket to fetch water* on the board. Elicit/ Explain other connections in the same way e.g. *You need straw to fix a bucket. You need a knife to cut straw. You need a stone to sharpen a knife,* etc.

5 Say *Now listen to the song and point to the words in the picture.* Play the recording.

6 Say *Why can't Henry mend his bucket?* (*because he needs a good bucket before he can mend the one with a hole in it*). Play the recording again to be sure that pupils understand the joke.

Step 2

1 If necessary, stick the A3 copy of worksheet 1 on the board, give each pupil their worksheet again and review the vocabulary and story from the song.

2 Point to Henry and Liza in the picture and elicit their names. Look at exercise 2. Explain that the list on the left is Henry's questions and problems and Liza's answers (jumbled) are on the right. Read through both lists, explaining vocabulary as necessary e.g. *cut, sharpen, blunt, wet.*

3 Put pupils in pairs to match the questions and answers, then play the recording for them to check. Then get different pupils to read out the sequence of questions and answers.
Key 1f, 2g, 3d, 4j, 5b, 6i, 7h, 8e, 9c, 10a

4 Say *Now let's sing the song.* Play the recording for pupils to sing along.

5 When pupils are confident, split the class into two groups to sing as Liza and Henry.

Step 3

1 Draw a tent on the board. Say *Who likes camping? What do you need when you go camping?* Write suggestions on the board including *bucket.*

2 Using the list on the board say e.g. *Why do we need a bucket?* Elicit the answer in the pattern *We need (a bucket) to (carry water).* Repeat with other items.

3 Stick the A3 copy of worksheet 2 on the board. Say *You're going camping. These are some things you might need.* Teach/Review vocabulary as necessary.

4 Put pupils into groups of three or four. Give each group worksheet 2. Say *You can only take ten of these things. Decide which ten things are the most important and say why.* Give pupils time to discuss. Monitor.

5 After about ten minutes, ask pupils to name one thing from their group's list and say why it's important e.g. *We need the rucksack to carry our clothes.* If time, vote on an agreed list of things to take on a class trip.

There's a hole in my bucket 1

1 Label the picture. Then listen and point.

water   bucket   stone   hole   ~~straw~~   knife   well

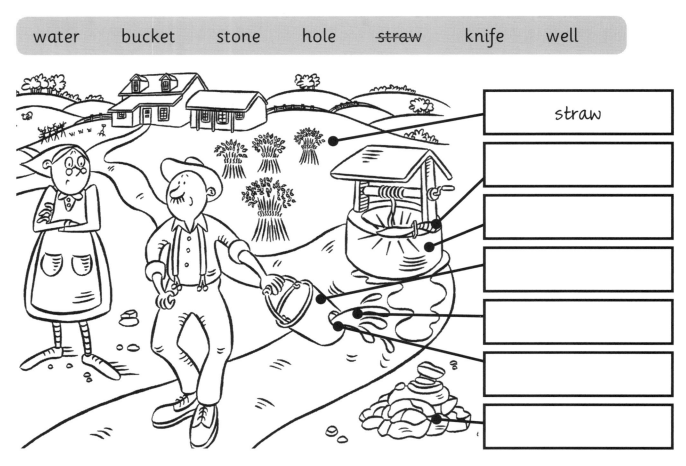

straw

2 Listen, read and match.

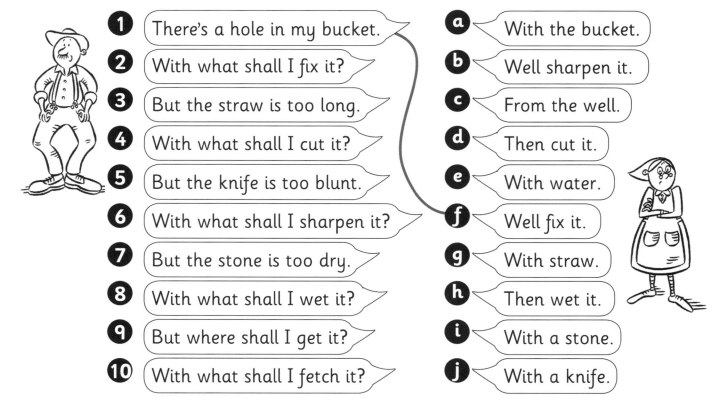

1 There's a hole in my bucket.

2 With what shall I fix it?

3 But the straw is too long.

4 With what shall I cut it?

5 But the knife is too blunt.

6 With what shall I sharpen it?

7 But the stone is too dry.

8 With what shall I wet it?

9 But where shall I get it?

10 With what shall I fetch it?

a With the bucket.

b Well sharpen it.

c From the well.

d Then cut it.

e With water.

f Well fix it.

g With straw.

h Then wet it.

i With a stone.

j With a knife.

There's a hole in my bucket 2

Talk to your friends and choose ten things to go camping.

tent ☐	rucksack ☐	bucket ☐	torch ☐
sleeping bag ☐	cooker ☐	chair ☐	bed ☐
food and drink ☐	penknife ☐	plate ☐	cup ☐
knife and fork ☐	spoon ☐	clock ☐	washbag ☐
book ☐	pen ☐	ball ☐	matches ☐

The Owl and the Pussycat

LANGUAGE FOCUS
words of a nonsense poem
following origami instructions
fold, crease, etc.

LEVEL 3

AGE RANGE 10–12

TIME
Step 1: 25 minutes
Step 2: 20 minutes
Step 3: 20 minutes

MATERIALS
🔘 **136** Lyrics p.143

Step 1
(Flashcards of all pictures on
worksheet 1)

Step 2
Worksheet 1 for each pupil

Step 3
A completed origami boat,
worksheet 2 for each pupil,
clean A4 paper for each
pupil, scissors and colouring
pens

**FOLLOW-UP
ACTIVITIES**
Class read and find out about
other poems by Edward Lear
(p.17)

Pupils use all the cut-out
characters and origami boat
to retell the story (p.15)

Step 1	Predicting and listening to the story
Step 2	Correcting mistakes in the words of the rhyme, saying the rhyme
Step 3	Making an origami boat for the Owl and the Pussycat

Step 1

1 Draw or stick the flashcard of the Owl and the Pussycat in the boat on the left of the board and introduce them. Write their names and *boat* next to them.

2 Say *We're going to listen to a story about the Owl and the Pussycat.* Teach/Elicit other vocabulary *turkey, guitar, ring, moon, money, sing, Piggywig, danced, sailed* by drawing or using the flashcards. Stick them on the board with the words next to them.

3 On the right of the board write *What did the Owl and Pussycat travel in?; Where did they go?; What did they take with them?; Who married them?; What did they need?; What was in the sky?; What did they do at the party?*

4 Check comprehension. Pupils work in pairs to guess the answers, using the pictures on the board. Elicit ideas. Then play the recording for pupils to check.
  Key in a boat / they went to sea / money, a five-pound note, a guitar / a turkey / a ring / the moon / danced
  Write the answers to the questions. Play the recording again for pupils to follow the story.

Step 2

1 Make mistakes for pupils to correct e.g. *Do you remember the Dog and the Pussycat?* (*No! The Owl and the Pussycat*). *They flew over the sea in a plane,* etc.

2 Give each pupil worksheet 1. Say *Some of these words are wrong. Listen.* Play the recording. Pupils cross out the wrong words. Check. (see 3 below)

3 Point to the labelled pictures. Say *These are the real words.* Give pupils time to try to match the labelled pictures to the text. Then say *Listen again and write the words.* Play the recording, stopping as necessary. Check.
  Key Verse 1 ~~Fruit bat~~ → Pussycat, ~~car~~ → boat, ~~chocolate~~ → money, ~~piano~~ → guitar;
  Verse 2 – ~~Horse~~ → Owl, ~~swim~~ → sing, ~~flew~~ → sailed, ~~Hennypen~~ → Piggywig, ~~ball~~ → ring;
  Verse 3 – ~~Chicken~~ → Turkey, ~~sun~~ → moon, ~~slept~~ → danced

4 Read the words with the class, explaining vocabulary e.g. *mince, quince* (meat and fruit). In this nonsense rhyme, many words e.g. *runcible, Bong-tree, Piggywig* are not real. Some, like *tarried* (went slowly), *shilling* (a small coin) and *fowl* (bird) are old-fashioned.

5 Say *Let's say it together.* Play the recording. Pupils follow, using their corrected text.

Step 3

1 Say *How did the Owl and the Pussycat travel in the story?* (*by boat*).

2 Show your ready-made boat. Say *You're going to make a paper boat like this. Look.* Make another boat, saying the instructions on worksheet 2. Teach *pattern, fold, in half, corner, crease, shape, front, back, triangle, press* and *flatten.* If possible, show how it floats.

3 Give each pupil worksheet 2 and read through the instructions with the class.

4 Give each pupil a piece of A4 paper. Make another boat, step by step, with pupils copying. Check at each stage.

5 When the boats are ready, elicit *Who went to sea in a pea-green boat?* Point to the Owl and the Pussycat on the worksheet. Pupils cut them out, colour them and put them in the boat.

6 Pupils can try sailing their boats.

The Owl and the Pussycat 1

Listen and correct the mistakes in the story.

a

Turkey

b

Pussycat

c

Owl

d

guitar

e

ring

f

boat

> Pussycat
> The Owl and the ~~Fruit-bat~~ went to sea
> In a beautiful pea-green **car**.
> They took some honey, and plenty of **chocolate**,
> Wrapped up in a five-pound note.
> The Owl looked up to the stars above,
> And sang to a small **piano**,
> 'O lovely Pussy! O Pussy my love,
> What a beautiful Pussy you are,
> You are, you are!
> What a beautiful Pussy you are!'

> Pussy said to the **Horse**, 'You elegant fowl!
> How charmingly sweet you **swim**!
> O let us be married! Too long we have tarried,
> But what shall we do for a ring?'
> They **flew** away, for a year and a day,
> To the land where the Bong-tree grows,
> And there in a wood, a **Hennypen** stood,
> With a **ball** at the end of his nose,
> His nose, his nose,
> With a ring at the end of his nose.

> 'Dear Pig, are you willing to sell for one shilling
> Your ring?' Said the Piggy, 'I will.'
> So they took it away, and were married next day
> By the **Chicken** who lives on the hill.
> They dined on mince, and slices of quince,
> Which they ate with a runcible spoon.
> And hand in hand, on the edge of the sand,
> They danced by the light of the **sun**,
> The moon, the moon.
> They **slept** by the light of the moon.

g

moon

h

money

i

sing

j

Piggywig

k

danced

l

sailed

1   Make an origami boat.

1  Use a rectangular piece of paper and draw a pattern on one side. With the pattern facing you, fold the paper in half, then open.	**2**  Fold the paper in half downwards. Now you can see the white side.	**3** Fold the top corners down to the vertical line in the centre.
4 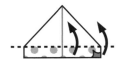 Fold the front paper at the bottom up. Do the same at the back. Crease it well.	**5**  Pull the sides of the shape out and flatten on the table to look like this.	**6** 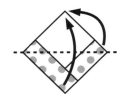 Fold the front of the paper up to the top to make a triangle. Do the same to the back.
7 Pull the sides of the shape out until the bottom points meet.	**8** Gently pull the top part of the shape, then press flat to make a boat shape.	**9**  Now you have a boat that you can sail on water!

2   Cut out the animals and tell the story.

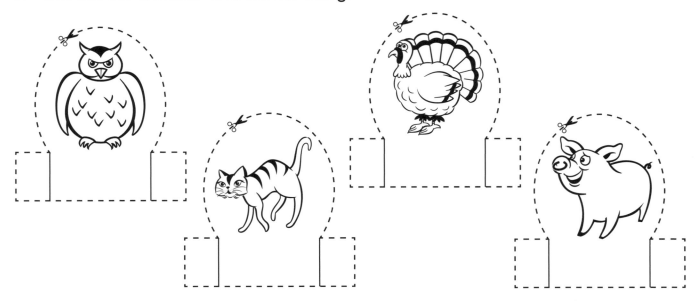

 Primary Music Box © Cambridge University Press 2010

Waltzing Matilda

3.12

LANGUAGE FOCUS
Australian English words
storytelling

LEVEL 3

AGE RANGE 10–12

TIME
Step 1: 25 minutes
Step 2: 25 minutes
Step 3: 25 minutes

MATERIALS
🔘 **137** Lyrics p.143

Step 1
Worksheet 1 for each pupil

Step 2
Worksheet 1 and words of
song (p.143) for each pupil

Step 3
Worksheet 2 for each pair
of pupils, scissors, (colouring
pencils)

FOLLOW-UP ACTIVITIES

Class start a list of common
slang words or differences
in British, American and
Australian English

Pupils act out the story from
the song (p.15)

> Step 1 Matching Australian and British English words, listening to the song
> Step 2 Ordering pictures in the story, singing the song in Australian (and British) English
> Step 3 Reading and ordering the story

Step 1

1 Draw a *boomerang* on the board and teach/elicit the word. Say *What country is it from?* (*Australia*). Tell pupils they are going to listen to an old Australian song.

2 Teach/Elicit the British English words a–h on worksheet 1. Explain about men in Australia in the old days, walking between sheep farms, looking for work.

3 Give each pupil worksheet 1. Point out the British English words on the right and the pictures and Australian English words on the left. Establish that many of the Australian words in the song are now old-fashioned. Say *Look at the example. In Australia a travelling farm worker was called a swagman. Now draw lines between the Australian and British words.* Check.
Key 1c, 2f, 3a, 4g, 5h, 6d, 7e, 8b

4 Say *Let's listen to the song. Look at the Australian words. Which one is not in the song?* Play the recording and check.
Key *boomerang*

5 Play the recording again. Pause each time an Australian word is mentioned e.g. *swagman* and *billabong* in line 1. Pupils call out the matching British English words.

Step 2

1 If necessary, give each pupil worksheet 1 again. Explain that the pictures in exercise 2 show the story of the song but are not in order. Elicit what is happening in each picture.

2 Pupils work in pairs to guess the order. Play the recording for them to check.
Key 1d, 2a, 3c, 4b

3 Establish the story of the song (*the traveller camps by a pond, tries to steal a sheep but is stopped by the landowner and policemen. To escape, he jumps into the water and drowns*).

4 Give each pupil the words of the song. Read them through with the class. Explain vocabulary as necessary. Establish that the traveller's ghost still haunts the pond.

5 Say *Let's sing the song.* Play the recording. Pupils sing along. (If time, sing again but replacing the Australian words with the British English ones.)

6 Say *The title of the song is Waltzing (dancing) Matilda. Who is Matilda?* Accept suggestions. (*the traveller's girlfriend or wife, the sheep*, etc.) Some people think that Matilda is the bedroll the traveller carries with him and dances with when he is alone!

Step 3

1 If necessary, get pupils to say what they remember about the story of Waltzing Matilda.

2 Put pupils into pairs. Give each pair a copy of worksheet 2. Say *This is the story of Waltzing Matilda. But the lines are in the wrong order.* Read the sentences and check vocabulary.

3 Give out scissors. Pairs of pupils cut out, read and order the text.

4 Check by getting pupils to read the story aloud.
Key d, g, a, f, b, j, i, c, e, h

5 (Make this activity more challenging by dividing the class into groups of ten and giving each pupil one sentence from the story. They have to organise themselves into the correct order.)

6 If time, pupils could illustrate the sentences for the story, to make a class storybook or poster.

1 Match the Australian and the British English words. Then listen and find the word that isn't in the song.

Australian English words

British English words

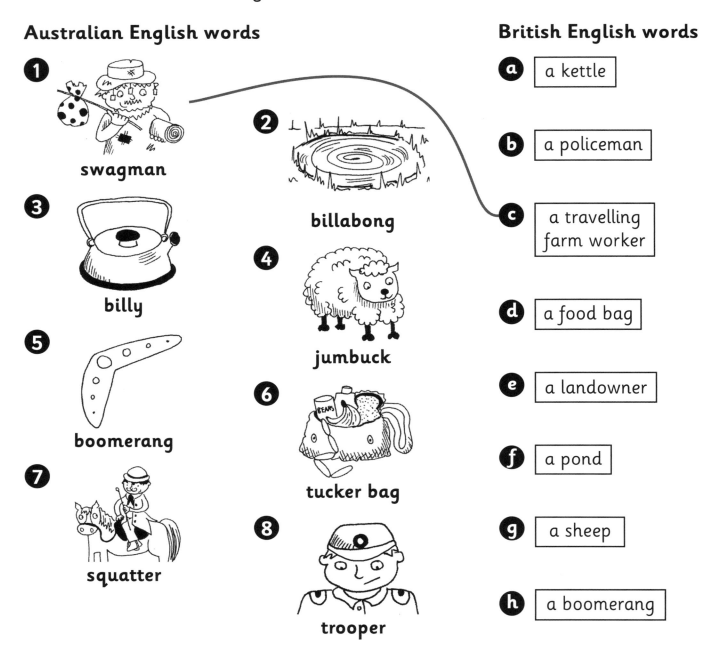

1 swagman

2 billabong

3 billy

4 jumbuck

5 boomerang

6 tucker bag

7 squatter

8 trooper

a a kettle

b a policeman

c a travelling farm worker

d a food bag

e a landowner

f a pond

g a sheep

h a boomerang

2 Listen and number the pictures.

a b c d

Cut out the sentences and put them in the correct order.

a He is hungry and thirsty. He boils some water in his kettle. But he doesn't have any food.

b He catches the sheep and puts it into his food bag.

c The traveller sees the policemen and wants to escape. He jumps into the water.

d A traveller is looking for somewhere to camp. He sees a nice place to camp by a pond.

e But the traveller can't swim. He drowns in the pond and dies.

f Then he sees a sheep. He wants to catch the sheep and eat it.

g He goes down to the pond. He makes a camp next to the water.

h The ghost of the traveller still lives in the pond.

i The landlord and the policemen go to the pond. They want to catch the traveller.

j But the landlord sees the traveller with his sheep. He is very angry and he calls the police.

Song lyrics

1.1 Ten in the bed

There are ten in the bed
And the little one says,
'Roll over. Roll over.'
So they all roll over and one falls out.

There are nine in the bed
And the little one says,
'Roll over. Roll over.'
So they all roll over and one falls out.

...

There's one in the bed
And the little one says,
'Goodnight'.

1.2 The wheels on the bus

The wheels on the bus go round and round,
round and round, round and round.
The wheels on the bus go round and round,
All day long.

The wipers on the bus go *swish, swish, swish* ...

The money on the bus goes *chink, chink, chink* ...

The mums on the bus go *chatter, chatter, chatter* ...

The dads on the bus go *ssh, ssh, ssh* ...

The bell on the bus goes *ding, ding, ding* ...

The wheels on the bus go round and round,
round and round, round and round.
The wheels on the bus go round and round,
All day long. All day long.

1.3 Hickory dickory dock

Hickory dickory dock,
The mouse ran up the clock.
The clock struck one (*bong!*)
The mouse ran down.
Hickory dickory dock.

Tick tock, it's one o'clock.
Tick tock, it's one o'clock.

Hickory dickory dock,
The mouse ran up the clock.
The clock struck three (*bong! bong! bong!*)
The mouse ran down.
Hickory dickory dock.

Tick tock, it's three o'clock.
Tick tock, it's three o'clock.

six o'clock …
eight o'clock …
ten o'clock …
twelve o'clock …

1.4 Dingle dangle scarecrow

When all the cows are sleeping,
And the sun is in its bed,
Up jumps the scarecrow,
And this is what he says.

Chorus
'I'm a dingle dangle scarecrow
With a flippy floppy hat!
I can shake my arms like this,
I can shake my legs like that!'

When all the hens are sleeping,
And the moon behind a cloud,
Up jumps the scarecrow,
And shouts out very loud.

'I'm a dingle dangle scarecrow
With a flippy floppy hat!
I can shake my arms like this,
I can shake my legs like that!'

1.5 The music man

Chorus
I am the music man,
I come from down your way,
And I can play!
What can you play?

I can play the piano,
the piano, the piano,
I can play the piano, pia-piano.

The vio-vio-violin, violin, violin,
Vio-vio-violin, vio-violin.

Boom boom, the big bass drum, the big
bass drum, the big bass drum,
Boom boom, the big bass drum, *boom*, the
big bass drum.

The saxo-saxo-saxophone, saxophone,
saxophone,
The saxo-saxo-saxophone, saxo-saxophone.

Ting, ting, ting, the triangle, the triangle,
the triangle,
Ting, ting, ting, the triangle, tria-triangle.

1.6 We wish you a Merry Christmas

We wish you a Merry Christmas,
We wish you a Merry Christmas,
We wish you a Merry Christmas,
And a Happy New Year.
Good tidings we bring to you and your kin.
We wish you a Merry Christmas,
And a Happy New Year.

Now bring us some figgy pudding …
And a cup of good cheer.
Good tidings we bring to you and your kin.
We wish you a Merry Christmas,
And a Happy New Year.

We won't go until we get some …
So bring some out here.
Good tidings we bring to you and your kin.
We wish you a Merry Christmas,
And a Happy New Year.

We wish you a Merry Christmas …
And a Happy New Year.
Good tidings we bring to you and your kin.
We wish you a Merry Christmas,
And a Happy New Year.

Song lyrics

1.7 Bingo

There was a farmer had a dog,
And Bingo was its name-o.
B-I-N-G-O!
B-I-N-G-O!
B-I-N-G-O!
And Bingo was its name-o!

There was a farmer had a dog,
And Bingo was its name-o.
(*clap*)-I-N-G-O!
(*clap*)-I-N-G-O!
(*clap*)-I-N-G-O!
And Bingo was its name-o!

There was a farmer had a dog,
And Bingo was its name-o.
(*clap, clap*)-N-G-O! ...
And Bingo was its name-o!

There was a farmer had a dog,
And Bingo was its name-o.
(*clap, clap, clap*)-G-O! ...
And Bingo was its name-o!

There was a farmer had a dog,
And Bingo was its name-o.
(*clap, clap, clap, clap*)-O! ...
And Bingo was its name-o!

There was a farmer had a dog,
And Bingo was its name-o.
(*clap, clap, clap, clap, clap*) ...
And Bingo was its name-o!

1.8 Old Macdonald had a farm

Old Macdonald had a farm, E-I-E-I-O.
And on that farm he had a cow, E-I-E-I-O.
With a *moo moo* here and a *moo moo* there,
Here a *moo*, there a *moo*, everywhere a *moo moo*!
Old Macdonald had a farm, E-I-E-I-O.

Duck – *quack quack* ...

Sheep – *baa baa* ...

Pig – *oink oink* ...

Cow – *moo moo* ...

Animal noises
cow, dog, sheep, cat, duck, horse, pig

1.9 If you're happy and you know it

If you're happy and you know it, clap your hands.
If you're happy and you know it, clap your hands.
If you're happy and you know it,
And you really want to show it,
If you're happy and you know it, clap your hands.

If you're happy and you know it, stamp your feet. …

If you're happy and you know it, nod your head. …

If you're happy and you know it, touch your nose. …

If you're happy and you know it, say 'I am', (*I am!*) …

1.10 There was an old lady

There was an old lady who swallowed a fly.
I don't know why she swallowed a fly!
Perhaps she'll die!

There was an old lady who swallowed a spider,
That tickled and tickled and tickled inside her.
She swallowed the spider to catch the fly.
I don't know why she swallowed a fly!
Perhaps she'll die!

There was an old lady who swallowed a bird.
How absurd, to swallow a bird!
She swallowed the bird to catch the spider,

That tickled and tickled and tickled inside her.
She swallowed the spider to catch the fly …
I don't know why she swallowed a fly!
Perhaps she'll die!

There was an old lady who swallowed a cat.
Fancy that, to swallow a cat!
She swallowed the cat to catch the bird.
She swallowed the bird to catch the spider,
That tickled …

There was an old lady who swallowed a dog.
What a hog, to swallow a dog!
She swallowed the dog to catch the cat.
She swallowed the cat to catch the bird.
She swallowed the bird to catch the spider,
That tickled …

There was an old lady who swallowed a cow.
I don't know how she swallowed a cow!
She swallowed the cow to catch the dog.
She swallowed the dog to catch the cat.
She swallowed the cat to catch the bird.
She swallowed the bird to catch the spider,
That tickled …

There was an old lady who swallowed a horse.
She's dead, of course!

Song lyrics

1.11 Here we go round the mulberry bush

Here we go round the mulberry bush,
The mulberry bush, the mulberry bush,
Here we go round the mulberry bush,
Early in the morning.

This is the way we wash our face,
Wash our face, wash our face,
This is the way we wash our face,
Early Monday morning.

This is the way we comb our hair …
Early Tuesday morning.

This is the way we brush our teeth …
Early Wednesday morning.

This is the way we put on our clothes …
Early Thursday morning.

This is the way we go to school …
Early Friday morning.

This is the way we tidy our rooms …
Early Saturday morning.

This is the way we stay in bed …
Early Sunday morning.

1.12 There was a princess long ago

There was a princess long ago,
Long ago, long ago,
There was a princess long ago,
Long, long ago.

And she lived in a big high tower,
A big high tower, a big high tower,
And she lived in a big high tower,
Long, long ago.

A naughty fairy waved her wand,
Waved her wand, waved her wand …

The princess slept for a hundred years,
A hundred years, a hundred years …

A great big forest grew around,
Grew around, grew around …

A handsome prince came riding by,
Riding by, riding by …

He took his sword and chopped it down,
Chopped it down, chopped it down …

He kissed her hand to wake her up,
Wake her up, wake her up …

So everybody's happy now,
Happy now, happy now.
So everybody's happy now,
Happy now.

2.1 The Hokey Cokey

You put your right arm in,
Your right arm out,
In, out, in, out, shake it all about.
You do the Hokey Cokey
And you turn around.
That's what it's all about!

Chorus
Oh, oh, the Hokey Cokey!
Oh, oh, the Hokey Cokey!
Oh, oh, the Hokey Cokey!
Knees bent, arms straight,
Ra, ra, ra!

You put your left leg in,
Your left leg out,
In, out, in, out, shake it all about.
You do the Hokey Cokey
And you turn around.
That's what it's all about!

You put your two ears in …

You put your one nose in …

You put your whole self in …

2.2 Kookaburra

(*short recording of kookaburra's call*)

Kookaburra sits in the old gum tree,
Merry, merry king of the bush is he.
Laugh, kookaburra! Laugh, kookaburra!
Great your life must be.

Kookaburra sits in the old gum tree,
Eating all the gum drops he can see.
Stop, kookaburra! Stop, kookaburra!
Leave some there for me.

Kookaburra sits in the old gum tree,
Counting all the monkeys he can see.
Hey, kookaburra! Hey!
That one's not a monkey, that one's me!

2.3 This old man

This old man, he played one,
He played knick-knack in the sun,
With a knick-knack, paddy whack,
Give a dog a bone,
This old man came rolling home.

This old man, he played two,
He played knick-knack on my shoe,
With a knick-knack, paddy whack,
Give a dog a bone,
This old man came rolling home.

This old man, he played three,
He played knick-knack in a tree …

This old man, he played four,
He played knick-knack on my door …

This old man, he played five,
He played knick-knack on my hive …

This old man, he played six,
He played knick-knack with my sticks …

This old man, he played seven,
He played knick-knack up to eleven …

2.4 We've got the whole world in our hands

We've got the whole world in our hands,
We've got the whole world in our hands,
We've got the whole world in our hands,
We've got the whole world in our hands.

We've got our brothers and our sisters in our hands,
We've got our friends and our family in our hands,
We've got people everywhere in our hands,
We've got the whole world in our hands.

We've got the sun and the rain in our hands,
We've got the moon and the stars in our hands,
We've got the wind and the clouds in our hands,
We've got the whole world in our hands.

We've got the rivers and the mountains in our hands,
We've got the seas and the oceans in our hands,
We've got the towns and the cities in our hands,
We've got the whole world in our hands.

We've got the whole world in our hands …

2.5 Do your ears hang low?

Do your ears hang low?
Do they wobble to and fro?
Can you tie them in a knot?
Can you tie them in a bow?
Can you flap them up and down,
As you fly around the town?
Do your ears hang low?

Does your tongue hang down?
Does it flop all around?
Can you tie it in a knot?
Can you tie it in a bow?
Can you flap it up and down,
As you fly around the town?
Does your tongue hang down?

Does your nose hang low?
Does it wiggle to and fro? ...

Do your eyes pop out?
Do they bounce all about? ...

2.6 I found a peanut

I found a peanut, I found a peanut,
I found a peanut yesterday.
Yesterday, I found a peanut,
I found a peanut yesterday.

Where did you find it, where did you find it,
Where did you find it, yesterday?
Yesterday, where did you find it?
Where did you find it, yesterday?

In a dustbin, in a dustbin,
In a dustbin, yesterday.
Yesterday, oh, in a dustbin,
In a dustbin, yesterday.

What did you do with it, what did you do with it?
What did you do with it, yesterday?
Yesterday, what did you do with it?
What did you do with it, yesterday?

Well, I ate it ...

What did it taste like ...?

It was disgusting ...

What did you do then ...?

I called the doctor ...

What did the doctor do ...?

He cut me open ...

What did he find there ...?

He found a peanut ...

Song lyrics

2.7 She'll be coming round the mountain

She'll be coming round the mountain when she comes. (*Toot toot!*)
She'll be coming round the mountain when she comes. (*Toot toot!*)
She'll be coming round the mountain,
Coming round the mountain,
Coming round the mountain when she comes. (*Toot toot!*)

Chorus
Singing aye aye yippy yippy aye. (*clap clap*)
Singing aye aye yippy yippy aye. (*clap clap*)
Singing aye aye yippy,
Aye aye yippy,
Aye aye yippy yippy aye. (*clap clap*)

She'll be driving six white horses when she comes. (*Yee hah!*) ...
She'll be wearing pink pyjamas when she comes. (*Lovely!*) ...
She will have to sleep with Grandma when she comes. (*Snore, snore!*) ...
We will all have some bananas when she comes. (*Yum yum!*) ...

2.8 The animals went in two by two

The animals went in two by two, hurrah! hurrah! ...
The animals went in two by two, the elephant and the kangaroo,
And they all went into the Ark, for to get out of the rain.

The animals went in three by three, hurrah! hurrah! ...
The animals went in three by three, the wasp, the ant and the bumblebee, ...

The animals went in four by four, hurrah! hurrah! ...
The animals went in four by four, the big hippopotamus stuck in the door, ...

The animals went in five by five, hurrah! hurrah! ...
The animals went in five by five, the frogs all jumping to keep alive, ...

The animals went in six by six, hurrah! hurrah! ...
The animals went in six by six, they loved the monkey because of his tricks, ...

The animals went in seven by seven, hurrah! hurrah! ...
The animals went in seven by seven, the crocodile thought he was going to heaven, ...

The animals went in eight by eight, hurrah! hurrah! ...
The animals went in eight by eight, the turtle thought he was coming late, ...

The animals went in nine by nine, hurrah! hurrah! ...
The animals went in nine by nine, the spiders and crabs in a long straight line, ...

The animals went in ten by ten, hurrah! hurrah! ...
The animals went in ten by ten, the last one in was the little red hen,
And they all went into the Ark, for to get out of the rain,
And they all went into the Ark, for to get out of the rain.

2.9 Jingle bells

(sounds of bells jingling)

Dashing through the snow,
In a one-horse open sleigh,
Over fields we go,
Laughing all the way.
Bells on bobtail ring,
Making spirits bright.
What fun it is to laugh and sing
A sleighing song tonight.

Oh, jingle bells, jingle bells,
Jingle all the way.
Oh, what fun it is to ride
In a one-horse open sleigh (*hey!*)
Jingle bells, jingle bells,
Jingle all the way.
Oh, what fun it is to ride
In a one-horse open sleigh.

2.10 Michael Finnegan

There was an old man named Michael Finnegan.
He had whiskers on his chinnegan.
They fell out and then grew in again.
Poor old Michael Finnegan.
Begin again …

There was an old man named Michael Finnegan.
He went fishing with a pinnegan.
Caught a fish and threw it in again.
Poor old Michael Finnegan.
Begin again …

There was an old man named Michael Finnegan.
He grew fat and then grew thin again.
Then he died and had to begin again.
Poor old Michael Finnegan.
Begin again …

There was an old man named Michael Finnegan.
He had whiskers on his chinnegan.
They fell out and then grew in again.
Poor old Michael Finnegan.
Begin again …

Stop!

Song lyrics

2.11 Row, row, row your boat

Row, row, row your boat,
Gently down the stream.
Merrily, merrily, merrily, merrily,
Life is but a dream.

Row, row, row your boat,
Gently down the stream.
If you see a crocodile,
Don't forget to scream!

Row, row, row your boat,
Gently down the river.
If you see a polar bear,
Don't forget to shiver!

Row, row, row your boat,
Gently float about.
If you see a waterfall,
Don't forget to shout!

Row, row, row your boat,
Gently to the shore.
If you see a lion,
Don't forget to roar!

Row, row, row your boat,
Gently in the bath.
If you see a spider,
Don't forget to laugh!

Row, row, row your boat,
Gently down the stream.
Merrily, merrily, merrily, merrily,
Life is but a dream.

2.12 Oranges and lemons

'Oranges and lemons,' say the bells of
St Clement's.
'You owe me five farthings,' say the bells
of St Martin's.
'When will you pay me?' say the bells
of Old Bailey.
'When I grow rich,' say the bells
of Shoreditch.
'When will that be?' say the bells
of Stepney.
'I do not know,' say the great bells of Bow.
Here comes a chopper to chop off your
head,
Chip, chop, chip, chop, the last man's dead!

3.1 In the Quartermaster's store

There are rats, rats, big as alleycats,
In the store, in the store.
There are rats, rats, big as alleycats,
In the Quartermaster's store.

Chorus
My eyes are dim, I cannot see.
I have not brought my specs with me,
I have not brought my specs with me.

There are goats, goats, eating all the oats,
In the store, in the store.
There are goats, goats, eating all the oats,
In the Quartermaster's store.

There are foxes, foxes, hiding in the boxes …

There are bears, bears, running down the stairs …

There are bees, bees, buzzing round the keys …

3.2 The house that Jack built

This is the house that Jack built.
This is the rat that ate the cheese
In the house that Jack built.

This is the dog that chased the cat
That killed the rat that ate the cheese
In the house that Jack built.

This is the farmer sowing his corn
That heard the cockerel crow at dawn
That woke the man who gave a yawn
That kissed the farm girl on the lawn
That milked the cow that had one horn
That scared the dog that chased the cat
That killed the rat that ate the cheese
In the house that Jack built.

Song lyrics

3.3 On top of spaghetti

On top of spaghetti,
All covered with cheese,
I lost my poor meatball,
When somebody sneezed.

It rolled off the table,
And onto the floor,
And then my poor meatball,
Rolled out of the door.

It rolled in the garden,
And under a bush,
And then my poor meatball,
Was nothing but mush.

The mush was as tasty,
As tasty could be,
And then the next summer,
Grew into a tree.

The tree was all covered,
All covered with moss,
And on it grew meatballs,
And tomato sauce.

So if you eat spaghetti,
All covered with cheese,
Hold on to your meatball,
If you start to sneeze.

3.4 Land of the silver birch

Land of the silver birch,
Home of the beaver,
Where still the mighty moose,
Wanders at will.

Chorus
Blue lake and rocky shore,
I will return once more.
Boom-diddy-ah-da, boom-diddy-ah-da,
Boom-diddy-ah-da, boom.

High on a rocky ledge,
I'll build my wigwam,
Close to the water's edge,
Silent and still.

My heart grows sick for you,
Here in the lowlands.
I will return to you,
Hills of the north.

3.5 London Bridge is falling down

London Bridge is falling down,
Falling down, falling down.
London Bridge is falling down,
My fair lady.

Build it up with wood and clay,
Wood and clay, wood and clay.
Build it up with wood and clay,
My fair lady.

Build it up with iron and steel …

Build it up with silver and gold …

Build it up with stone so strong …

Wood and clay will wash away …

Iron and steel will bend and bow …

Silver and gold will be stolen away …

Stone so strong will last so long …

3.6 The green grass grew all around

There was a hole in the middle of the ground,
The prettiest hole that you ever did see.
Well, the hole in the ground,
And the green grass grew all around and around,
The green grass grew all around.

And in that hole there was a tree,
The prettiest tree that you ever did see.

Well the tree in the hole,
And the hole in the ground,
And the green grass grew all around and around,
The green grass grew all around.

And on that tree there was a branch …

Well the branch on the tree,
And the tree in the hole,
And the hole in the ground,
And the green grass …

And on that branch there was a nest …

Well the nest on the branch,
And the branch on the tree,
And the tree in the hole,
And the hole in the ground,
And the green grass …

And in that nest there was a bird …

Well the bird in the nest,
And the nest on the branch,
And the branch on the tree,
And the tree in the hole,
And the hole in the ground,
And the green grass …

And on that bird there were some feathers …

Well the feathers on the bird,
And the bird in the nest,
And the nest on the branch,
And the branch on the tree,
And the tree in the hole,
And the hole in the ground,
And the green grass grew all around and around,
The green grass grew all around.

3.7 As I was going to St Ives

As I was going to St Ives,
I met a man with seven wives.
Every wife had seven sacks,
Every sack had seven cats,
Every cat had seven kittens.
Kittens, cats, sacks and wives,
How many were going to St Ives?

3.8 The twelve days of Christmas

On the first day of Christmas,
My true love sent to me:
A partridge in a pear tree.

On the second day of Christmas,
My true love sent to me:
Two turtle doves and a partridge in a pear
tree.

On the third day of Christmas,
My true love sent to me:
Three French hens, two turtle doves and a
partridge in a pear tree.

On the fourth day of Christmas – four
calling birds …
On the fifth day of Christmas – five gold
rings …
On the sixth day of Christmas – six geese
a-laying …
On the seventh day of Christmas – seven
swans a-swimming …
On the eighth day of Christmas – eight
maids a-milking …
On the ninth day of Christmas – nine ladies
dancing …
On the tenth day of Christmas – ten lords
a-leaping …
On the eleventh day of Christmas – eleven
pipers piping …

On the twelfth day of Christmas,
My true love sent to me:
Twelve drummers drumming,
Eleven pipers piping, …
And a partridge in a pear tree.

3.9 When I first came to this land

When I first came to this land,
I had no money in my hand.
So I got myself a shack.
I did what I could.
And I called my shack *Break my back*,
But the land was sweet and good.
I did what I could.

When I first came to this land,
I had no money in my hand.
So I got myself a farm.
I did what I could.
And I called my farm *Muscle in my arm*,
And I called my shack *Break my back*,
But the land was sweet and good.
I did what I could.

When I first came to this land,
I had no money in my hand.
So I got myself a horse.
I did what I could.
And I called my horse *Lame, of course!*
And I called my farm *Muscle in my arm*,
And I called my shack *Break my back*,
But the land was sweet and good.
I did what I could.

When I first came to this land,
I had no money in my hand.
So I got myself a cow.
I did what I could.
And I called my cow *No milk now*,
And I called my horse *Lame, of course!*
And I called my farm *Muscle in my arm*,
And I called my shack *Break my back*,
But the land was sweet and good.
I did what I could.

Wife – *Love of my life …*
Daughter – *Fetch the water …*
Son – *My work's done …*

3.10 There's a hole in my bucket

Henry

There's a hole in my bucket, dear Liza,
dear Liza.
There's a hole in my bucket, dear Liza,
a hole.

With what shall I fix it, dear Liza,
dear Liza?
With what shall I fix it, dear Liza,
with what?

But the straw is too long …
With what shall I cut it? …
But the knife is too blunt …
With what shall I sharpen it? …
But the stone is too dry …
With what shall I wet it? …
But where shall I get it? …
With what shall I fetch it? …
There's a hole in my bucket …

Liza

*Well fix it dear Henry, dear Henry, dear
Henry.*
Well fix it dear Henry, dear Henry, fix it.

*With straw, dear Henry, dear Henry,
dear Henry.*
*With straw, dear Henry, dear Henry,
with straw.*

Then cut it …
With a knife …
Well sharpen it …
With a stone …
Then wet it …
With water …
From the well …
With the bucket …

Song lyrics

Primary **Music Box**

3.11 The Owl and the Pussycat

The Owl and the Pussycat went to sea
In a beautiful pea-green boat.
They took some honey, and plenty of
money,
Wrapped up in a five-pound note.
The Owl looked up to the stars above,
And sang to a small guitar,
'O lovely Pussy! O Pussy my love,
What a beautiful Pussy you are,
You are, you are!
What a beautiful Pussy you are!'

Pussy said to the Owl, 'You elegant fowl!
How charmingly sweet you sing!
O let us be married! Too long we have
tarried,
But what shall we do for a ring?'
They sailed away, for a year and a day,
To the land where the Bong-tree grows,
And there in a wood, a Piggywig stood,
With a ring at the end of his nose,
His nose, his nose,
With a ring at the end of his nose.

'Dear Pig, are you willing to sell for one
shilling
Your ring?' Said the Piggy, 'I will.'
So they took it away, and were married
next day,
By the Turkey who lives on the hill.
They dined on mince, and slices of quince,
Which they ate with a runcible spoon.
And hand in hand on the edge of the sand,
They danced by the light of the moon,
The moon, the moon.
They danced by the light of the moon.

3.12 Waltzing Matilda

Once a jolly swagman camped by a
billabong,
Under the shade of a coolibah tree,
And he sang as he watched and waited till
his billy boiled,
'Who'll come a-waltzing Matilda with me?'

Chorus
'Waltzing Matilda, waltzing Matilda,
Who'll come a-waltzing Matilda with me?'
And he sang as he watched and waited till
his billy boiled,
'Who'll come a-waltzing Matilda with me?'

Down came a jumbuck to drink at that
billabong.
Up jumped the swagman and grabbed him
with glee.
And he sang as he shoved that jumbuck in
his tucker bag,
'You'll come a-waltzing Matilda with me.'

Chorus Waltzing Matilda … And he sang as
he shoved that jumbuck in his tucker bag …

Down came the squatter, riding on his
thoroughbred,
Up came the troopers, one, two, three.
'Where's that jolly jumbuck you've got in
your tucker bag?
You'll come a-waltzing Matilda with me.'

Chorus '… Where's that jolly jumbuck you've
got in your tucker bag?' …

Up jumped the swagman and jumped into
the billabong.
'You'll never catch me alive,' said he.
And his ghost may be heard as you pass by
that billabong,
'You'll come a-waltzing Matilda with me.'

Chorus … And his ghost may be heard as
you pass by that billabong, …

Primary Music Box © Cambridge University Press 2010 **PHOTOCOPIABLE** **143**

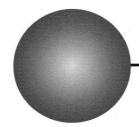

CD track listing

Track		Song
1		Introduction
2	1.1	Ten in the bed
3	1.2	The wheels on the bus
4	1.3	Hickory dickory dock
5	1.4	Dingle dangle scarecrow
6	1.5	The music man
7	1.6	We wish you a Merry Christmas
8	1.7	Bingo
9	1.8	Old Macdonald had a farm
10	1.9	If you're happy and you know it
11	1.10	There was an old lady
12	1.11	Here we go round the mulberry bush
13	1.12	There was a princess long ago
14	2.1	The Hokey Cokey
15	2.2	Kookaburra
16	2.3	This old man
17	2.4	We've got the whole world in our hands
18	2.5	Do your ears hang low?
19	2.6	I found a peanut
20	2.7	She'll be coming round the mountain
21	2.8	The animals went in two by two
22	2.9	Jingle bells
23	2.10	Michael Finnegan
24	2.11	Row, row, row your boat
25	2.12	Oranges and lemons
26	3.1	In the Quartermaster's store
27	3.2	The house that Jack built
28	3.3	On top of spaghetti
29	3.4	Land of the silver birch
30	3.5	London Bridge is falling down
31	3.6	The green grass grew all around
32	3.7	As I was going to St Ives
33	3.8	The twelve days of Christmas
34	3.9	When I first came to this land
35	3.10	There's a hole in my bucket
36	3.11	The Owl and the Pussycat
37	3.12	Waltzing Matilda